The Millionaire Software Developer

Paul Smyth

BookLocker

Saint Petersburg, Florida

DISCLAIMER

This book details the author's personal experiences with and opinions about starting and growing a software development business. The author is not a licensed legal, investment or accounting professional.

The author and publisher are providing this book and its contents on an "as is" basis and make no representations or warranties of any kind with respect to this book or its contents. The author and publisher disclaim all such representations and warranties, including for example warranties of merchantability and business startup and growth advice for a particular purpose. In addition, the author and publisher do not represent or warrant that the information accessible via this book is accurate, complete or current.

The statements made about products and services have not been evaluated by the U.S. government or any other government. Please consult with your own legal, accounting, investment, or other licensed professional regarding the suggestions and recommendations made in this book.

Except as specifically stated in this book, neither the author or publisher, nor any authors, contributors, or other representatives will be liable for damages arising out of or in connection with the use of this book. This is a comprehensive limitation of liability that applies to all damages of any kind, including (without limitation) compensatory; direct, indirect or consequential damages; loss of data, income or profit; loss of or damage to property and claims of third parties.

You understand that this book is not intended as a substitute for consultation with a licensed investment, legal or accounting professional. Before you begin any change your lifestyle in any way, you will consult a licensed professional to ensure that you are doing what's best for your situation.

This book provides content related to starting and growing a software development business. As such, use of this book implies your acceptance of this disclaimer.

TABLE OF CONTENTS

INTRODUCTION

WHO IS THIS BOOK FOR?

This book was written for all those people working in the software industry who dream of starting their own business and being their own boss. Whether you want to escape your current job, your employer, your boss, or whether you have a burning ambition to have your own business, this book will show you the path to follow to achieve the freedom you long for.

The book is primarily targeted at those people who want to use their software skills to build a software development business.

If your goal is to use your development skills and experience to work on technology projects and to build a successful and profitable business, then this book is for you.

It doesn't matter whether you have development skills, analysis skills, project management skills, consulting skills, or implementation skills. The important thing is that you are keen to be your own boss, pulling the strings, and making all the key decisions in a software development business.

If you want to choose the technologies and platforms that you work with and to build a successful business around those technologies, then this book is for you.

If you want to choose where you work from so that you get more quality time with your family, then this book is for you.

If you're fed up making others wealthy with your skills, then this book is for you.

If you feel underappreciated and underpaid for the value you bring to your employer and wish that you could do something about it, then this book is for you.

If you want to create a future where there are no upper limits on your earnings and where you can create **real wealth** and **financial freedom** for you and your family, then this book is for you.

If you're concerned that your age is working against you and you are fearful about holding down a high-paying job in the future, then this book is for you.

If you like the idea of starting a business but you're afraid to take the next steps because you have an overwhelming fear of failure, then this book is for you.

If you're nervous about starting a business because you have no idea how you would win customers for your business, then this book is for you.

If you're holding back from starting because you think you need a lot of money to start a business, then this book is for you.

If you already have a software development business (or previously had one) and you are struggling to reach seven figures and grow the business, then this book is for you.

If you think starting a business is *too* risky, then this book is for you.

In the course of this book, you will learn that starting a business doesn't have to be *too* risky and that you don't need a lot of money to get started.

Even though I've written the book to show how you can bootstrap your own software development business from nothing and grow it into a multi-million-dollar company, you can still apply most of what you will learn from it if you're lucky to have backing for your venture.

WHO IS THIS BOOK NOT FOR?

Firstly, this is not a get-rich-quick book. If you think you can become a millionaire in the next few weeks by following the teachings in this book then you will be sadly disappointed.

Launching a business and growing it to seven figures and more will take real effort. You will have to work hard to get there. It will not happen overnight.

If you're going to run a successful business you're going to have to open your mind to a whole new set of ideas and you will have to be willing to learn several new skills.

You're going to have to learn about sales and marketing, finance, negotiation, recruitment, and other business disciplines. Be ready to embrace this.

If this isn't you, or you think you already know everything you need to know to be able to run a business, then this book is definitely not for you.

If you're the type of person who hates engaging with people, especially strangers, then you really should think twice about setting up your own business.

If you think that selling is the work of the devil and that marketing is a waste of money, then you're probably not cut out to be a businessperson.

If you think customers are a pain in the ass, and should only be tolerated as a last resort, then this book is not for you.

If you want to build a successful, sustainable business you're going to have to engage with people.

In the services world, people buy from people not
from businesses.

You will not be successful if you cannot interact with others in a reasonably confident manner. The more you're comfortable with this the more successful you can be.

WHAT QUALIFIES ME TO TEACH THIS STUFF?

If you live in the technical world you will know that masses of books get written on all sorts of topics.

What has always intrigued me is the number of books that get published for a new technology on the same day that technology appears on the market.

Take any major new version of SQL Server or Oracle as an example. On the day of the release of either, you can probably buy ten or more books about the new version.

Granted, these products would have been in beta for some time. It is, however, extremely unlikely that all these books were written by people with real production experience with the database.

Typically, what happens is that most of these books just regurgitate the release notes and the documentation into a friendly book format.

Ultimately there is no substitute for experience and so the best books are usually those written some time after the product has been released and used in production for real-world use cases.

I mention this because I want you to know that this is not a book rushed out five minutes after I have set up my own software company. It has taken me a lot of real-world learning to get to this point.

So, to answer the question *"What qualifies me to teach this stuff?,"* my reply is this: 35 years of experience in the software industry with more than 20 of those years spent as a CEO bootstrapping a multi-million-dollar software development business from a standing start.

THE JOURNEY THAT LED TO THIS BOOK

I first started programming in COBOL on a DEC PDP 11 in 1981. Most of you reading this will never have heard of a PDP 11 but many experts regard it as the most successful minicomputer ever.

As the '80s moved on the IBM PC started to make inroads into business. It was becoming realistic for small businesses to own PCs and to use them for word processing, spreadsheets, and other office tasks.

Even though the big salaries in those days were in the mainframe and minicomputer markets, the fast-growing PC market was a more attractive proposition to me.

I can't honestly say that I had a great vision at that time and that I knew how big the PC industry would become, but there was a definite buzz about it, and it seemed an exciting place to be.

My first foray into the PC world came when I joined a startup run by a husband-and-wife team.

We developed accounting software for small businesses in MS-BASIC. We provided a turnkey solution, supplying SuperBrain PCs running CPM, the standard operating system at that time.

The software was supplied as two floppy disks—a program disk and a data disk.

After three years there, during which time I also learned 'C', I relocated and went to work for a software house that supplied software to the investment-management world.

This was a big step up for me. It was a far more professional environment with more rigor and standards, and I learned a lot during my time there.

I quickly settled in, and within a year, I was promoted to a team-lead position. I was eventually appointed to lead the team in building a new investment-management product.

Shortly after this, the company was acquired by one of the big players in the investment management software sector.

The culture of the company changed, and I decided to move on. I was well paid at the time and it was hard to match my salary in other positions.

I landed a job as Head of Software Development at a software company that was a division of a property consultancy.

I took a big drop in salary because I was excited by the opportunity to run the development department. I was also told that if things went to plan I would be offered the opportunity to join the board.

I quickly made a positive impact in my new role and I got most people on my side. I also built a good relationship with the managing director and other board directors.

It was the time when 4GLs were all the rage and we decided to adopt Progress 4GL as our development environment. We had a lot of success with Progress for about four years, but they missed the boat when GUIs took over following the success of Windows 3.

I knew that we had to change ship or potentially go out of business, so I recommended to the board that we adopt Visual Basic & SQL Server as our preferred development environment.

I suggested Visual Basic because a lot of corporates were adopting it at that time and we already had the skills in-house. Thankfully, the board agreed with me.

Not long after switching to Visual Basic we won two multi-million-dollar contracts with two global food organizations.

We then won two more big contracts, one with a major bank, the other with a major retailer. These successes vindicated my decision to jettison Progress.

Within a year of joining, I was appointed as a director and I was eagerly learning how a company operates and how to play a part at the board level. I was also taking on more responsibility for managing a growing development team.

As we grew and went after bigger projects, I also started to play a key role in the sales process.

I worked in tandem with the sales director, helping to present to new prospects and to build our technical credibility. As my confidence grew, I thrived in this environment. There was always a great buzz when we won new customers.

I spent seven years at this company, but as time went by my mind began to think about starting my own company.

My wife would occasionally ask me about our pension arrangements (I didn't have any!) and I would respond *"Don't worry. I'll have my own company one day and that will be our pension."*

However, time kept passing by with no action on my part. But the following year two pivotal events happened within a few months of each other.

In September of that year, I went to a conference where I heard one of the most brilliant talks I've ever heard.

In a talk entitled *"Just Say Yes"*, Craig Low of IBM spoke about excellence in customer service. It was so inspiring and made me realize that by focusing on excellence in customer service you could build a successful company.

I still have the recording of that talk on my phone and I listen to it every so often as a reminder to stay focused on the customer experience.

Then, three months after that conference, I hit my 40th birthday. That same morning, I had a real awakening.

I realized how quickly time had gone by since I was 30 and that if I kept procrastinating I would be 50 before I knew it.

That was the day I made the decision that I was going to start my own company and I was going to make customer service the number one priority.

Strangely, I didn't have any fears or doubts. I instinctively knew that it was the right thing to do. I had an inbuilt confidence that I could make it work.

The following week I approached a colleague from our sales team and told him of my plans. I asked him if we would like to join me and he immediately said yes.

Within a few short months, we launched our company and embarked on our entrepreneurial journey.

GETTING TO HERE

This book is the result of the experience I gained over the following 20 years running and growing our company through multiple technological changes and multiple economic cycles.

> *You can pick up this book safe in the knowledge that this is not the result of a cookie-cutter process to churn out another "How to" book.*

Along the way, there were many highlights and a few lowlights. There were many long hours and much hard work as we built the business.

There were also some periods of stress but thankfully these were few and far between. Most of the stress I endured was because we were so busy.

We rapidly built the business into six figures, and within 18 months we were on a seven-figure run-rate, billing around $85k per month. From there we continued building the business into multiple seven figures of revenue per annum.

We were very profitable, and we generated significant cash surpluses. This enabled us to take large dividend payments (one of which I used to pay off my six-figure mortgage) and to build a substantial war chest to protect us from any economic shocks that might come our way.

It was a hugely satisfying journey and we had a lot of fun too. I've never once regretted my decision to start the company.

Well, I can think of one: I shouldn't have procrastinated for as long as I did, and I should have started the business years earlier.

If there's one thing that I want this book to achieve it's that I hope it inspires and motivates readers like you to have the confidence to take the plunge and start your own software development business.

I want to encourage you to stop procrastinating and get started. There is an exciting future in front of you provided you take that first step and start your own business.

Know this. You can never build real wealth by working for somebody else.

The best way to build lasting wealth, and to achieve financial freedom for you and your family, is to have your own successful business.

Forget about MBAs and degrees. They are not a prerequisite to starting a business. I didn't have either of those.

The key ingredients you need are solid development skills, a willingness to take action and a commitment to stick at it. If you have those then the lessons in this book will help you increase your chances of success.

Now, read on to discover how you can build your own successful and profitable software development business.

FUNDING THE BUSINESS

COMMON ROUTES TO FUNDING

Only a very small proportion of businesses ever get external backing to enable them to launch their company. The vast majority of small businesses are started by people raising their own funds.

There are several ways that you can fund a new business. Here are some of the common ways used by bootstrappers:

- Using your savings
- Using money from family and/or friends
- Raising a bank loan
- Remortgaging your house
- Credit cards

Of these, I most favor the combination of savings and credit cards. This is how I started my company.

With this combination, I had estimated that we could survive for the best part of a year with little or no business.

Sure, there's some risk involved but that's also true of all the other options. If your business doesn't take off and you can't pay back your credit cards, then you risk bankruptcy and bad credit ratings.

But starting a business is all about taking calculated risks.

The more savings you have the less you will need to lean on the credit cards. However, not everybody has the luxury of lots of savings, so using a combination of both can be a good way to get started.

The option I favor the least is using a bank loan. When I started my business, I did everything possible to avoid putting my house on the line.

The last thing you need when starting a business is to be stressing out about losing your house and, even worse, having your spouse or life partner getting stressed out about it.

You're unlikely to get a bank loan for a new services business anyway without putting up collateral—and that usually means your house.

Banks are notoriously reluctant to back a new business no matter how good your plan looks.

Never be under any illusions. Retail banks are
not risk-takers.

You'd probably be able to raise the money more easily if you told them it was being used for a new kitchen because they can understand how that would increase the value of their collateral (your house).

Re-mortgaging your house is a better option, but you should only do this if you have plenty of equity in the property and are sure that you can afford to make the subsequent higher repayments.

Bear in mind that if your business doesn't take off and you can't make the repayments then you stand to lose your house.

Probably one of the most common ways to raise funds is to get them from family or friends.

I'm not a fan of taking this route as it carries the potential for damaging family relationships or friendships if things go wrong.

For many people, this might be the easiest option for quickly raising the cash to get started but I would only recommend doing it if the person lending the money can afford to lose it without it having a major impact on their life.

The worst outcome of using this funding route is that your business fails, and you become bankrupt and at the same time, your lender's life is ruined by the loss of the money. And if that person is close to you then you may have damaged your relationship irreparably.

OTHER SOURCES OF FUNDING

When I started my business there was no such thing as crowdfunding as we know it today. Peer-to-peer lending was also unknown.

Nowadays there are multiple routes to raising funding such as AngelList, Kickstarter, Indiegogo, Crowdfunder, etc. The list grows longer every day.

As a general rule, I would say that these funding options lend themselves better to people building tangible products or apps rather than those trying to grow a services business.

THE LEAST RISKY SOURCES OF FUNDING

In the early days of my business I deliberately avoided trying to get work by poaching any customers from my previous employer. I knew that if I had done that I would've faced litigation.

However, I did feel free to approach ex-customers and people I had met during my time there. One of these contacts subsequently became one of my biggest customers, but more about that later.

If you're in a position to ethically approach a customer, ex-customer, or some other contact who could give you work, then that is a great way to kick-start your business.

Launching a business with guaranteed work is the easiest way to fund your start.

Another great way to start, and this may surprise some of you, is to approach your existing employer. Really!

If your employer values you, and you have a good relationship with them, then they might be willing to buy services from your new company.

If you're an important cog in their wheel, or you have some critical knowledge or experience that they will find hard to replace, then it gives them some continuity even if they lose you as a full-time employee.

This option could work well for both parties and it would enable you to launch with a guaranteed income stream.

However, you must be careful not to get sucked into working full-time for them whereby you had little opportunity to grow your company.

You need to retain the right to choose who does the work and to be in control of the time spent doing it. Otherwise, you would effectively become a full-time contractor to them with little capacity to grow a business.

ADOPT A FRUGAL MINDSET

Bootstrapping a company is not just about funding your business through its early stages. It's also about the sacrifices you'll need to make to get your business off the ground.

Living lean during the early months of your business enables you to build up the cash reserves in the business. This is vital to ensure you build a solid business.

When I started my business I gave up a well-paid job as a company director. I also gave back a company car.

During the early months of the business, my wife and I lived very frugally as I concentrated on building up the business. We stopped going out to restaurants regularly. My wife cut back on our weekly shopping by looking for bargains, using coupons, and checking prices to ensure we got good deals.

I would estimate that we reduced our discretionary living costs by up to 50% at the time.

Now if the thought of doing this is horrific to you, then I would question if you are truly committed to your business and if you have the right entrepreneurial mindset.

Remember, your goal is to build wealth by creating a successful business over the long term. In the short term, you need to make some sacrifices to get there. And always remember that these sacrifices are for *your* benefit. Never lose sight of that goal.

You are no longer helping somebody else get rich. You are building your future. Keep your eye on that ball.

There's a well-known saying about this:

> *"Entrepreneurship is about living a few years of your life like most people won't so you can spend the rest of your life like most people can't."*

GO SOLO OR WITH A PARTNER?

MY EXPERIENCE OF PARTNERING

I always knew that I wanted a partner when I started my business. I had no solid basis for knowing why this would be a good thing but intuitively I knew it would be better for the business.

After 20 years of partnership, I can say that I'm glad I partnered, as we built a very successful business together.

That isn't meant to dissuade you from starting a business on your own. Thousands of people choose to do exactly that every year and many will go on to become a success. However, it is much easier to bootstrap a business with a good partner because a good partnership can bring a broader mix of skills to the table that will enable you to accelerate your growth.

When I started my business I had many years of technical skills and management and board-level skills with some sales skills thrown in. My partner brought some sales skills along with excellent customer relationship skills. Together we formed a strong team that worked well in front of customers. We had different but complementary personalities, which meant that we slipped naturally into our roles: me as CEO and my partner as the business development director.

The advantage this gave us was that in the early days, when I was the breadwinner doing most of the billable technical work, he was able to continue looking for more customers. This enabled us to grow much quicker than if I had started on my own.

WHY PARTNER?

Over the years I have seen a number of reports[1] showing that companies are more likely to grow bigger and faster when started by more than one person. Of course, the big issue with a partnership is deciding who to partner with.

Most successful partnerships are started by friends or colleagues, i.e., people who knew each other before going into business together. Partnerships such as Paul Allen and Bill Gates at Microsoft, Steve Jobs and Steve Wozniak at Apple and Larry Page and Sergey Brin at Google are good examples of this.

It might be stating the obvious, but if you're going to start a business with a partner then you need to be quite sure that you can work together through both good and bad times.

MAKING A PARTNERSHIP WORK

Trust is paramount in any partnership. Do you know your partner well enough to have full trust in them? Without mutual trust, you are doomed from the get-go. Is their integrity unquestioned? Is their character representative of the brand you plan to have?

If you have any misgivings about them, trust your gut. If someone seems slippery, or bogus, or a jerk, don't ignore it.

You also need to ensure that you have a shared vision for the business because no partnership will survive if you have fundamental differences. Make sure that you understand each other's financial goals, life goals, and that you mutually agree on the aims.

---

[1]Shailendra Vyakarnam, "Management: Breaking the myth of the one-man band," *The Independent*, April 6 1994,
https://www.independent.co.uk/news/business/management-breaking-the-myth-of-the-one-man-band-1368257.html

A key decision in any partnership is how to split the equity. Are you all going to have an equal split?

Who's contributing the most startup capital? Should they get more/less equity?

Is it your vision and they are coming on as minority shareholders?

A two-person partnership is the one I favor.

In my experience, a two-person 50/50 partnership is quite a stable split—but only if the two of you get on well together. The result is that it means you are both equally committed.

Obviously, if you can retain 51% or more of the equity then this gives you majority control, which can work to your advantage in the future, particularly when it comes to selling the business.

As a rule, I would advise against having too many founding partners. Two is good and is very common in business. More than three can lead to problems.

If you have too many people with an equal say in matters, then it becomes much harder to achieve consensus and to make quick decisions. It also increases the chances that there will be more disputes as the company grows.

If you do decide to go into business with one or more partners, then make sure that you establish clear roles for everybody right from the get-go.

Somebody must be CEO and the boss. Who is that? Do *not*, I repeat, do *not*, have joint CEOs. That just doesn't work. If you have difficulty agreeing who should be the CEO then that's an early warning sign that the partnership might not be a good one. Everybody should also be clear about what's expected of them.

The work equity expectations should be set from the beginning. If these are not set correctly, this will quickly lead to a breakdown in the partnership. One of you will feel that the other isn't pulling his or her weight, and it will eventually create a lot of problems.

If your partner wants to go to the beach or play golf every day while you want to work seven days a week to grow the business, things aren't going to work out.

The best time to go into a partnership is right at the beginning of the journey because all partners become equally invested in the business. It's certainly much harder, but not impossible, to bring in a partner at a later stage in the business.

I've got two friends who each started their own separate businesses. After running their businesses for some years, they thought that they would be able to grow the business faster if they had a partner.

They each took on a partner but, in both cases, the partnership failed, and they ended up working on their own again.

Both owners found it very difficult to operate with less than the 100% control of the business they had become used to, and relations with their partners slowly but surely went sour.

PARTNERSHIPS CAN GO WRONG

One note of caution about partnerships.

You might start off in a good partnership but as time passes you could find that life and business circumstances will cause you to drift apart.

If there's a big age difference between partners, then over time this will begin to create different needs for both sides, and cracks in the relationship can begin to appear.

> *Partnerships can last a long time but eventually changing*
> *circumstances can lead to differences.*

Life events, such as the arrival of children or divorce, can change people's outlook. The partner you started the business with, and with whom you had shared goals, may no longer have the same vision as you.

I would certainly recommend that you get a partnership or shareholder's agreement put in place at an early stage to provide some protection against disputes and disagreements, but this is can only deal with some of the issues that could arise.

Many partnership disputes are resolved by one partner buying out the other. Reaching agreement on this can be tricky as each side's valuation of the deal is often widely different.

In such cases, it pays to bring in a third-party mediator to help reach agreement.

Ultimately, the potential partnership problems that you might encounter down the road shouldn't put you off having a partner.

You are far more likely to build a bigger company if you don't try to do it on your own.

GOING SOLO IS OK TOO

So, what happens if you don't have an ideal partner or if you don't like the sound of partnering?

Then just start the business yourself. You can still build a seven-figure company on your own. Plenty of people have done it.

As you grow, you can start building an executive team to work with you while still retaining majority control of the business.

It's far better to retain full control than to end up with a bad partner.

To help you make the right choice for you, here is a list of advantages and disadvantages of partnering versus going solo.

ADVANTAGES OF GOING SOLO

1) You can follow *your* vision. As the sole owner, your vision for your company will be completely uncompromised. You can set the direction, the culture, the branding, etc. This is important when first starting up, as the strength of your

vision and your commitment to it will be crucial to your success.

2) You get to be your own boss. As the sole owner, you don't have to ask anybody else if you want to do something. You can be spontaneous. You can just go ahead and do it when you want. You also don't have to answer to somebody who doesn't respect you.

3) You make all the key decisions. As the sole owner, you get to choose the company name, the office location, the technology you want to work with, the customers you want to work with, etc. You have unquestioned control of the operation. You'll make all the important decisions on pricing, marketing, staffing, expansion, etc.

4) The profits are all yours. As the sole owner, you don't have to share the proceeds from your business. You get to decide what to do with the profits: keep them in the business as reserves, reinvest them, or take them out as dividends.

5) You can sell the company when *you* want to. As the sole owner, if you get an offer for the business, you can choose to sell or keep the company without needing other shareholders to agree. And if you sell the business one day, then the full payout is yours.

DISADVANTAGES OF GOING SOLO

1) You have to fund the business on your own. As the sole owner, you have to find the capital to start and operate the business. It can be harder to raise startup capital if you don't have access to your own resources.

2) It can get lonely. As the sole owner, you have nobody to brainstorm with or bounce ideas off. When it gets tough it's easy to get down when you have nobody to share it with.

3) You have no checks and balances. As the sole owner, you get to make the decisions but what if they're not good decisions? It's easier to make mistakes if you don't have somebody offering a balanced counterview.

4) Lack of skills. As the sole owner, you might not have some skills that are needed in the business. You can learn these skills over time, but initially, this might hold you back.

5) It's harder to grow. As the sole owner, the business relies on you for so much. It's easy to spread yourself too thin and constrain growth. Statistically fewer one-man businesses get to seven figures than multi-owner businesses. Yes, it's possible but harder.

ADVANTAGES OF PARTNERING

1) Greater access to funding. Funding the business is no longer entirely down to you. A partner should also bring capital into the business.

2) More skills in the business. Very few individuals have all the skills and knowledge needed in a business. A partner can bring additional skills, knowledge, and experience that you might not have. They can undertake tasks that you might not be good at.

3) Sharing the burden. Partners offer mutual support and companionship, and they can also be there to share your start-up problems. It can be stressful and lonely at times

running a business alone. With someone else, you can feel like you are in it together.

4) You can get more done, faster. Partners share the workload and help get things done faster than if everything fell on one person to do. You can split responsibilities so that each partner focuses on different areas of the business.

5) Better, more effective decision-making. A partner will bring different perspectives on problems. It often helps to be able to see different points of view. Being able to look at problems from many angles can help to achieve better and/or more creative solutions: more people means more perspectives.

6) You can grow bigger, faster. Statistically, more partnerships will reach seven figures than sole proprietorships. You can also generate bigger profits.

DISADVANTAGES OF PARTNERING

1) Less control and autonomy. You won't have full control over the company and the decisions made. You won't be able to do your own thing and you won't always get your own way.

2) More scope for disputes. You won't always agree with your partner(s). Are you willing to accept this? Are you able to disagree without throwing the towel in?

3) Conflicting goals. You may end up with different ambitions and goals for the business. You may have differences in personal aims. You may have different views on personal rewards versus investment in the business.

4) Conflicting views on work equity. You may disagree about how much work each partner should put in. A partner might only be willing to work a certain number of hours per week. There may be resentment when the reward is not seen as fairly matched by effort.

5) Slower decision making. Decision-making can be slower, as you have to win consensus. Some things may never happen because the partner(s) can't agree.

PREPARE YOUR FAMILY

MAKE SURE YOU HAVE SUPPORT

Many entrepreneurs overlook the impact that starting a new business will have on their personal life. Most people are so gung-ho about launching their business that they never give it a second thought.

In many ways, that's a good thing because the one thing an entrepreneur needs is plenty of optimism and energy.

The last thing that is needed is to become overly analytical and to see so many negatives that you fail to start your business.

However, there is one very important party to consider when starting your business and that is your family.

Your spouse or life partner and your children (if you have any) will be hugely affected by your changing circumstances. I recommend that you prepare them for these changes.

> *I was lucky that when I started my business I had a very supportive wife who was willing to make sacrifices to our lifestyle to enable me to pursue my dream of having my own business.*

I can't stress enough how important it is to have an understanding spouse or life partner during your startup phase when you're having to work your butt off to get the business off the ground.

For most of the first 18 months of the business, I was working seven days per week doing 80–100 hours every week.

Even though I was working mainly out of my house, I had less downtime with my wife than I had when I was an employee working in an office 20 miles away.

I was getting up before 6 a.m. every morning and, after showering, going straight to my desk to start work.

If I wasn't visiting a customer, my average day consisted of two short breaks for lunch and dinner and then straight back to my desk.

Most evenings I worked until around midnight, occasionally pulling a later one if I had a deadline to meet.

My social life dwindled to almost nothing during that early period of the business. All my focus was on growing the business and doing whatever it took to achieve that.

My only let-up was when family members came to stay, which forced me to spend some downtime with them.

Through all of this, my wife never complained. She understood what I was trying to achieve, and she helped in any way she could.

She was always willing to give up time to man the phones if we were out of the office. She regularly drove us to the train station when we had to go to customer meetings, and she'd be there to pick us up when we returned.

There was never any pressure from her on me to spend less time working. I think if I had had that pressure it would have made life much more difficult.

IT CAN BE TRICKY WITHOUT SUPPORT

A friend of mine, on the other hand, didn't have it quite so easy when he started his business. His wife was less understanding than my wife. She was rarely willing to help when he needed it and there was always an underlying sense of pressure from her. She was a natural worrier and was uneasy at the risky nature of the endeavor.

To be fair, they had two young children so their circumstances were different from mine, but the lack of support my friend got from his wife made his life a lot harder in the startup phase.

I know from conversations with other business owners that having the support of your spouse or life partner is vital to your personal well-being and the well-being of the business.

*The startup phase of a new business is intense. You don't
need additional pressure from your personal relationships
adding to the mix.*

I recommend that you work hard at explaining your plans to your spouse or life partner and listen to their concerns and then address them as best as you can before launching your new venture.

It sure is easier to start a business when they are on your side right from the get-go.

WORKING FROM HOME

THE DREAM SCENARIO

Many people are driven to start a business because they want not only to be their own boss but to also have the freedom to be able to work from home.

There's no doubt that working from home has many advantages. These include:

- No commuting and no travel costs
- Flexibility to work at any time of the day
- More time with your family
- There can be tax advantages

As you will have read in the previous chapters, I started my business from my house and I had the "luxury" of working from home.

But, as I discovered, it worked in reverse to the way that I would have expected.

The convenience of having the office available 24 hours of the day was a big advantage to me, as I was able to put in a big number of billable hours each week and to generate a lot more income.

If I'd had to spend time commuting, then I would have had additional costs and less billable hours.

But there's a darker side to working from home.

IT CAN BE A DOUBLE-EDGED SWORD

Having the office right next to you can also make it very difficult to stop working. I was working every waking hour of the day.

Even at weekends, I was drawn to the office and I would work long hours catching up on admin stuff such as the bookkeeping, timesheets, invoicing, etc.

When I first started thinking about having my own business, I also thought that it would enable me to play more golf. I reckoned that I'd be able to leave work early or take some time off to go play 18 holes whenever I fancied it. What a foolish thought that was!

In the first two years of the business, I played less golf than I'd ever played at any time over the previous 10 years. But I don't regret that. Golf was no longer a priority for me. My focus was on growing the business and so I spent most of my time working at my desk in my home office. Much as I loved golf (and still do) I didn't miss it at the time. I had something more important to concentrate on.

IT MAY NOT BE THE RIGHT CHOICE

Working from home won't suit everybody. You have to be very disciplined about focusing on your work. It is all too easy to be distracted by children, household chores, outside interests, etc. You have to know yourself well and decide if that's the best environment for you.

I know some people who don't want to work from home because they don't like the isolation that comes with it. They prefer to be in a social work environment where they have contact with other people.

I also know other people who feel that their family life isn't conducive to having a good home working environment. If you have young children, then it might be difficult to create a good space where you can concentrate on your work without distractions.

Software development is a very cerebral activity and you need a good environment to be able to concentrate on your work. If you can't create this environment for yourself at home, then you should think twice about having your office there.

THE BEST REASON TO WORK FROM HOME

There is one overwhelming reason to consider working from home particularly in the early stages of building your business. And that is the cost saving.

Keeping control of your costs is one of the golden fundamentals when bootstrapping a business.

If you can save costs on office space by working from home, then that is one less expense to worry about and will help you preserve your cash reserves.

As our business grew, I ended up giving up two rooms in our house to our growing team of developers. At about the two-year point I had eight developers coming into my house every day.

Eventually, my very tolerant wife cracked and started pushing me to move the business out of the house. The final straw for her was when one of the developers marched into our kitchen to make a cup of coffee and got in the way of her cooking. His disregard for her space was the tipping point.

I probably should have moved the business out of the house much earlier, but I was being ultra-cautious in keeping our expenses under control. I needed the push to make the final decision so when the time came to go I wasn't unhappy at moving the business out of the house and into an office.

By the time we moved out we had built up substantial cash reserves, so the move to rented office space was very low risk.

Besides, we were very busy and still recruiting so the move was inevitable.

The great thing about starting the business from my house was that we got to prove to ourselves that the business would fly and would be profitable before we incurred a major expense such as rented offices.

Once we did decide to move we knew we had the cash to easily cover the additional expense.

TIPS FOR WORKING FROM HOME

During my time working from home, I learned a number of things. Here are my top tips:

- Create a quiet, distraction-free area to work in.
- Make sure you have proper furniture. It's worth spending money on a good chair. I recommend Aeron chairs.
- Set boundaries. Let your family and friends know that you are working and that it's not okay to keep interrupting you.
- Take regular breaks to keep your head fresh and get your body moving. Get some exercise. Run, walk, cycle, swim, etc.
- Stay out of the kitchen. Avoid the temptation to continually graze. It's very easy to pile on the pounds.

FIRE YOURSELF ASAP

DELEGATE OR FAIL

One of the biggest skills you need as a business owner is the art of delegation.

You *must* become an expert at delegation if you are going to succeed in business.

> *Never fall into the trap of believing that others can't do the job as well as you can. That is a guaranteed route to failure.*

If you're going to grow a seven-figure business, you must realize that you can't do that on your own. You will be building a team to help you get there and you must allow that team to do the work you hired them for.

Don't take on work that you can easily and cheaply hire people to do. It's just bad use of your time. Delegate or outsource work whenever you can. This will reduce the workload on you and enable you to focus on growing the business.

Your goal is to fire yourself from as many roles as quickly as possible.

You can't be the business owner and main breadwinner for long. If you don't change you will hold back growth.

I made this mistake in my early days. I continued to be the highest revenue earner in the company up until about the 18-month mark. I didn't realize then that this was slowing our growth.

On top of that, I was burning myself out. I was becoming exhausted because I was doing so much development work as well as trying to run the business.

When I stopped being the main developer and started focusing on being the CEO and growing the business, we quickly grew as we hired more developers who could do more billable work than I could.

When you're bootstrapping a business, everybody has to take on multiple roles and everybody must do whatever it takes to get the business off the ground.

However, once you've acquired your first couple of customers the time will come when you need to devote all your energies to growing the business to seven figures.

So, make sure to recruit great people who you can delegate to and then fire yourself from as many roles as quickly as possible.

BRANDING

WHY BRANDING IS VITAL

Building your brand should always be top of mind. It's one of the main things that separates a successful seven-figure services business from mom and pop type businesses.

When I talk about branding, I'm talking about the image your company gives off to a prospect.

Your branding is the messaging that leaks from you and your business like radioactivity.

It's all about creating the right impressions with prospects and customers *before* they've even met you. You want to do everything you can to prevent them from negatively pre-judging you.

Get your branding right and you will stack the odds in your favor.

If you pay attention to the small details, you can position your business to grow to seven figures and beyond. If you ignore them, you can retard the growth of your business.

You can just as easily look like a seven-figure business as a mom-and-pop business. So why wouldn't you spend some time getting the little details correct? By positioning your business correctly, you put yourself in the frame to win better customers and bigger projects and to propel your business to a higher level.

So, let's look at some of the things you can do to ensure that you project the right image.

YOUR COMPANY NAME

I'm a big believer that choosing a good company name is very important.

I think that it's worth putting in some effort to come up with a name that will project the right image for your company.

A name can quickly create three reactions from prospects even before they know you.

1) **Positive:** they like the name or it projects an image that they like, or it identifies you as being right in their space. It might also arouse their curiosity

2) **Neutral:** the name doesn't cause any particular reaction. It's just another company name

3) **Negative:** the name creates a negative image of the company for some reason. Maybe it divides opinion or isolates a certain part of your audience. Maybe it projects the image of a company they don't want to work with or a company that's too small for them

Very few companies have a name that immediately evokes positive reactions. Most company names are in the neutral zone. Even big names such as eBay, Google, Amazon, etc., have names that didn't evoke any reaction in the beginning. They could have been selling anything.

The key thing to avoid is having a name that could cause your intended audience, or even some of them, to have a negative reaction.

It's okay to have a name that turns off some people as long as those people are *not*, and are never likely to be, your intended prospects/customers.

TIPS FOR CHOOSING A COMPANY NAME

Tip 1) I would strongly advise against naming the company after yourself. Your name means nothing to your target audience and having an eponymous company name can also make it harder to sell the company further down the road. It can also make it harder for you to let go of the reins because it has your name attached. You might not see that as important now, but 5, 10, 20 years down the road, when you want to sell the business or step away from it, you will not want your reputation damaged if new owners/management run the business more aggressively or less ethically than you would.

Tip 2) Think about how you want to be perceived by your target customers. Do you want to appear as small or as a one-man band or do you want to portray a bigger more professional image? If it's the latter, and that's what I recommend, then calling your company something like "Mike's Development Services" will limit people's perception of your company. When you try to land seven-figure deals this can work against you as you could be perceived as too small.

Tip 3) Think about where you see the future of your company. Will your name still be representative of the business in a few years? Can you have a name that gives the appearance of the company you want to be?

Tip 4) Take care that the name doesn't pigeonhole your business in a way that could restrict your growth. For example, if you're doing Java development today but your plan might involve developing in other languages in the future, then a name like ABC Java Developers could pigeonhole you in the minds of your prospects and make it hard for you to win business in other areas. See the next tip for a counter to this.

Tip 5) If you're targeting a niche audience, and you don't have plans to expand beyond that audience, then a name that strengthens your appeal to that niche can be a good thing.

Tip 6) You might be operating locally now but could you see your business expanding to other locations? If yes, then be careful about naming your business after your current location, as that will have little relevance to your audience in the future and may restrict your chances of expansion.

Tip 7) Be careful about being too cute or too trendy when coming up with a name. Something that might seem clever or trendy now could soon become obsolete and you could be left with a dated or unfashionable company name.

Tip 8) Avoid the use of superlatives or redundant descriptors. Avoid words like "best," "quality," "top," etc. These are hackneyed phrases and can set you up for a fall. You're more likely to evoke a negative reaction.

Tip 9) Don't make it difficult for people to pronounce or remember your name. Using numbers or punctuation marks in your name makes it difficult to explain and remember.

Tip 10) Avoid initials. It's almost impossible to have a unique set of initials. Research[2] has shown that invented words or real words are 40% easier to remember than initialized words.

Tip 11) Make sure that you can acquire a matching domain. Avoid domains with punctuation or numbers. Grab other matching domains (e.g. .net, .io, etc.) while you can. This can help protect your name and brand and avoid confusion with other companies.

Tip 12) Make sure that you claim matching social media accounts on Twitter, Facebook, LinkedIn, etc.

Tip 13) Stay legal. Don't try to impersonate another company or brand. Beware of misspellings of existing business names or brands. This can make your site seem suspicious for spamming or phishing. Naming your company or domain similar to an existing business may cause copyright or abuse complaints against you, potentially resulting in legal action.

YOUR BUSINESS STRUCTURE

First, let me say that when it comes to structuring your business you will need some legal advice.

Each country and jurisdiction has its own laws and regulations, so I can't offer definitive advice, as I'm not a legal advisor. What I can offer is some guidelines about incorporating your business so that it

---

[2]"How to Name (or Rename) Your Company: 3 Steps & Mistakes to Avoid" https://www.marketingsherpa.com/article/how-to/3-steps-mistakes-to-avoid

supports your brand and positions your business in the most favorable way possible.

I chose to incorporate my business because it positioned me well in the eyes of prospects and customers.

I don't like sole proprietor status, as it projects the image of a small company and that's not the goal of this book. I want you to build a seven-figure (and more) business, so start by setting up like a seven-figure business.

In the U.S. my personal preference would be to set up as an S Corp. In the UK and Ireland, I would opt for being a Limited company. Other countries will have similar types of companies.

There are both legal and tax implications in setting up a company so please ensure that you *get advice* on this before making a final decision.

YOUR REGISTERED ADDRESS

One thing you have to do with any business is to register a business address.

I would strongly advise against using your home address as the registered address even if you intend to work from home.

Using your home address portrays you as a small company. It doesn't look good if you're trying to win big projects and it is likely to restrict your growth.

Big companies will always check you out. They will look up the relevant business register to find out about you. Don't give them a chance to have a negative impression about you even before you've won the business.

My advice is to use a registered office service. These are available everywhere and don't cost a fortune. You can get an address in a building that makes you look like a serious company right from the get-go.

YOUR OFFICE ADDRESS

Your registered business address and your office address are not necessarily the same thing. You can be registered with one address but operate from a different address.

In fact, over time you could move offices several times while keeping the same registered address.

In the same way that I don't recommend using your home address as your registered address, I also don't recommend that you use your home address as your office address.

Once again this is all about perceptions. You don't want prospects getting preconceived negative opinions of you before you've even met them.

So, even if you work from home it pays to use a service address for your office address.

Buy mail forwarding as well so that all post sent there gets routed to you.

When people are checking you out, they will go to Google to see where you're located. Don't let them see your home.

The service address should be one that looks like an office
building when viewed in Google street view.

Another good reason to use a service address is that there are privacy concerns.

If you use your home address as your business address, that means you need to provide your home address whenever a customer or a vendor needs contact information. Also, using your home address may compromise your family's privacy. The last thing you want is for a disgruntled customer or vendor to be able to show up at your doorstep.

YOUR EMAIL ADDRESS

The quickest way to give away the fact that you're a small business (maybe even a one-man show) is to use a public email domain (gmail.com, yahoo.com, comcast.net, etc.) as your business email address. That's a real rookie mistake and will prevent you from being taken seriously if you're looking to win large projects.

When setting up your email addresses pay attention to the little things that could give away that you're still only a small business.

An email address such as *mike@yourdomain.com* suggests a small company because you can only have one Mike in the company.

Instead, use a future-proof format that suggests you could have lots of staff e.g.,

> *firstname.lastname@yourdomain.com*
> *lastname+initial@yourdomain.com*

Make sure that you have multiple email addresses for different purposes even if they all route to you at the beginning e.g.,

support@yourdomain.com
info@yourdomain.com
sales@yourdomain.com

Use these different email addresses on your website in the appropriate places.

When it comes to business, being cute, smart, or wacky with your email addresses can be a turn-off for many prospective buyers. Leave that for your personal accounts.

And finally, be careful to avoid email addresses that could be divisive (e.g., references to race, creed, gender, religion, politics, etc.)

TAKING PHONE CALLS

You will need to publish a landline number for your business. Seven-figure companies don't use cell phone numbers as their main point of contact so you shouldn't either.

You can easily buy a virtual landline number even if that routes to your cell phone, and make sure to subscribe to a phone-answering service so that calls are taken professionally when you're not available.

Remember also that background noises, such as children crying, dogs barking etc., will detract from the professional image you're trying to create. This is another reason why it's important to have a separate, quiet space to operate from when you're working from home.

YOUR LOGOS AND ARTWORK

It's now so easy and cheap to get quality artwork done so there's no reason why you can't look like a seven-figure business right from the get-go.

You can use outsourcing sites like https://www.fiverr.com/ or https://99designs.com to get bids for artwork and logos to your specifications.

Or use a site like https://www.freelogoservices.com to pick a design from an online library and download the files immediately after payment.

You can then use the same artwork to get business cards done. Make sure that you have a supply of these when you go to meet prospects or attend events.

YOUR WEBSITE

Your website is your shop window. Every prospect will check it out at some stage, so it needs to support your seven-figure branding.

It should look like you are a seven-figure business. Compare it to your big competitors. Don't be afraid to model your site on other well-known sites in your industry. As long as you don't directly copy them you'll generally be okay. Do *not* build it yourself no matter how good you think you are.

This is your first test of delegation. You're wasting valuable time if you try to develop it yourself. You can get a website built very quickly and cheaply using outsourcing sites such as https://www.fiverr.com/.

> *Your job is to focus on the website content. Leave the*
> *tech stuff to others.*

I recommend that you use WordPress for your site. It's the most popular CMS. It's free and it has tons of plug-ins. There are loads of cheap resources that will help you with it. It's a no-brainer.

Pick a professional theme that fits your brand. I like the Divi theme. It's easy to set up and to manage content. There are some great child themes to start from. Find a WordPress developer with Divi experience on an outsourcing site. It can cost less than $100 to get a site with multiple pages set up.

Make sure that your site is responsive and mobile-friendly. This is essential, as most content is now consumed on mobile devices and Google can penalize your site if it's not mobile-friendly.

Use the logos and artwork you already chose. Choose a corporate font and apply it consistently through your site. Once the site is set up and running you can concentrate on adding the content.

If you can, choose an ISP that can offer to host the site on SSDs. This gives you the best performance for your dollars.

One thing that's a giveaway that you're an amateur organization, and will lose you credibility instantly, is if your website is full of typos and spelling mistakes. The golden rule is this: spellcheck, spellcheck, spellcheck. Spelling and typo errors will instantly turn people off. Nothing is worse than a shoddy site with lots of errors. Seven-figure companies pay attention to these matters. Make sure you do.

How can people trust you to do good work if your
website is full of typos and errors?

You won't even know that you've lost potential business. Site visitors will just go away without you even being aware of it. Don't let this happen to you.

Implement a four-eyes policy as a minimum. Have at least two different people check the page(s) over before publishing. You can even outsource the proofing to an expert using services like https://www.fiverr.com/. Additionally, make sure that all links work as expected. Put in 404 handling so that even if a link doesn't work you can still route them somewhere useful.

DEFINE YOUR CULTURE

WHY CULTURE IS SO IMPORTANT

Your company culture is a key factor in determining whether you will succeed in the long term. A poor culture will eventually undermine your business and ultimately the business is likely to fail.

The reason that culture is so important is that it drives so many aspects of the business.

Culture defines your company's internal and external identity. It can attract the right employees or customers to your business. But it can also repel them if they don't like what they see or hear.

Culture can also help you keep good people. And in the hi-tech world, keeping good people is tough when they have so much choice.

> *Money is rarely the top reason that people stay with a company, but culture can be a primary reason.*

Culture enables people to bond around a common purpose and to function as a high-performing team. When you have a clear culture, it sets expectations for how people should work together in the interests of the company.

Culture also establishes the moral and ethical tone of your business. It defines what behaviors are acceptable and what behaviors will not be tolerated. Without good ethics and morals, you will never retain employees or customers and your business will be doomed.

IT'S YOUR DECISION

The great thing about setting up your own business is that you get to create a culture that aligns with your core values.

Do you want it to be casual, formal, clubby, hierarchical, flat, adhocracy, etc.? It's your choice.

You can choose whatever style suits you and the company you want to build.

You can decide

- What the company stands for
- What the company values are
- What the company ethics are
- What standards you expect
- What the acceptable behaviors at work are

NON-NEGOTIABLES

When I set up my business I had some non-negotiables concerning the things that embodied the core values that I believed would contribute to our success.

- Treat employees as I'd like to be treated
- Having satisfied customers is the central focus of the business
- Quality work is the only work worth doing
- Respect both colleagues' and customers' time
- Everybody does what it takes to get the job done
- Discrimination will not be tolerated

Around those core components, I also ensured that we paid people well and that we celebrated our successes by funding travel trips around Europe. We offered our people flexi-time options. We had a relaxed dress culture when not meeting customers. We gave people bonuses when the company did well, etc.

All these things added up to making our company a good place to work and helped us retain employees for longer periods than many other companies.

YOU ARE THE LEADER

Whatever culture you decide on never forget that you are the leader.

Employees will look to you for guidance and leadership. You will not always know the answer, but it's important that you take decisive action when required.

Regardless of how collaborative a culture you have, there will be many times when you, as the leader, will have to make a decision. Sometimes there will be tough decisions to be made. Don't shirk from this responsibility. Make decisions in the best interests of the company and you will be right most of the time.

Strong companies always have strong leaders. Leaders who are clear about where the company is heading and who are not afraid to make decisions.

Strong doesn't mean being a bully. That type of management style is not one that can last. Strong means being ready to make decisions even when you know those decisions won't be popular with some people.

Your job is not to make decisions based on whether they are popular or not. Your job is to make decisions that are right for the company. Most of the time those decisions will be popular but sometimes they won't.

Make fairness your guiding principle. Treat people fairly and you will be respected even if they don't like your decision.

BEWARE OF A NEGATIVE CULTURE

Culture, good or bad, exists in every company. In many companies, it just develops organically. However, it's often the case that the culture that develops is not a positive one. If you're not careful, this is what could happen in your company. Therefore, it's vital that you lay the foundation for the culture you want and don't let a negative culture develop that isn't representative of your core values.

If the wrong culture develops you will end up dealing with a lot of stressful situations and will ultimately struggle to make a success of the business.

TASKS TO COMPLETE

1) Start thinking about what your core values are.

2) Define the type of culture you'd like your company to have.

3) What does your company stand for?

4) What are the ethics of the company?

5) What rules of work do you want to have?

6) What are the behaviors that you want to enable and encourage?

7) What are the unacceptable behaviors in your company? Those are easy to see: discrimination, rudeness, lateness, etc.

BUSINESS PLANNING

WHY YOU NEED A PLAN

Here's a bold statement that I regularly make:

*"Most business plans are a waste of time, but business
planning is essential."*

Over the years I've spent countless hours, days, and weeks working on business plans. I've learned two key things during that time:

1. A business plan is an essential tool to help you to grow your business

2. Your business will grow in ways that you never planned for. No business plan I wrote ever worked out according to the plan.

But there's no getting around it. You must have a plan. Without a plan, you won't know where you're heading.

You won't be able to communicate your direction to those around you.

You won't be able to get funding or raise debt if you plan to go that route.

You won't even be able to tell whether your business is going to be viable.

Writing a business plan is daunting for most entrepreneurs. Many people who start businesses have never been involved in writing business plans before and many will also never have seen a formal business plan.

Even though I've been involved in numerous business plans over the years it is still an activity that I struggle to get enthusiastic about.

It can be a real slog to get all your thoughts and ideas down and to wrap them in a meaningful plan that stands up to scrutiny.

My natural instinct is to plow straight ahead and just get working and to solve the problems we encounter along the way.

But I also know that this is not always the right approach. No matter how much I dislike the planning process I know it has to be done.

Despite this, I still caution people about getting so bogged down in writing a plan that it stops them from launching their business.

Spending months and months writing a business plan is not the way to go. If you take this route, then you will likely end up with paralysis through analysis.

THE BEST PLAN IS A SIMPLE PLAN

If you are trying to raise finance from an institution, then you will be expected to provide an in-depth plan for the investors. But for bootstrappers, my advice is to focus on writing a simple business plan that captures all the key elements that will drive your business over the coming 18–24 months. My recommendation is to follow the process outlined by Kraig Kramers in his book "CEO Tools" (https://ceotools.com).

I'm a big fan of the One-Page Business Plan concept. If you can capture the key elements required for this, then you will have a good basis for launching.

The reason I like the One-Page Business Plan is that it focuses your mind on the key elements of the plan and stops you from getting bogged down in the minutiae. It is far less daunting than trying to write a 50-page plan with loads of details that you can only guess at right now.

DETAILED PLANS ARE A WASTE OF TIME

You're a bootstrapper. You're starting something from nothing. You're building a software development startup.

You can't accurately predict how many customers you will find and what services they'll require or how much they will buy from you.

You need to be adaptable and agile in the startup phase. You can't plan for this with any accuracy.

Many people get caught up in trying to execute their business plan when the fact of the matter is the market doesn't care about your business plan.

The only thing that matters is what you discover and apply out there in the real world beyond your office. Most successful startups end up doing something different than they originally intended or envisioned because they adapt to the market.

> *A business plan is not a business. Every day spent writing a business plan is a day wasted trying to generate revenue.*

Unless you're pitching for funding the only person who needs to see the plan is you (and your partner, if you have one).

People spend weeks and months building a plan and never look at them once the business gets going. This is what happens in real life.

THE ONE-PAGE BUSINESS PLAN

The key elements you'll need to capture in the One-Page Business Plan are:

1) Your vision for the business

2) The services you will offer

3) The customers you will serve

4) Your value proposition

5) Your route to market

6) How you will earn revenue

To be able to write your One-Page Business Plan you have to define each of these elements in more detail.

At this stage, it's more important to get through these steps relatively quickly and to get into the market to test your ideas.

As stated above, your plan will change as you begin to win customers. You'll have to adapt to market feedback.

Once you're up and running with some customers then you can come back and expand the plan.

In the next chapters, we'll look at each of these elements.

YOUR VISION

WHERE ARE YOU HEADING?

A vision statement says what the organization wishes to be like at some point in the future. It's an articulation of its major goals and ambitions.

A vision statement is like a photographic image of your future business, which gives your business shape and direction.

Visions should provide a sense of aspiration; they should stretch the imagination.

WHY YOU NEED A VISION

Building a successful seven-figure business requires a collective effort. You will not get there on your own. You will need to build a team to help you get there.

A clear vision will help you recruit the right people onto the bus. A compelling vision will act as an attractor to people who want to make a difference in their lives.

Once you've got the right people on the bus your vision should inspire them to go the extra mile and help make your business a success.

Having a clear vision will also help you make the right decisions. It will help you avoid getting distracted by opportunities that are not ideal for your business.

EXAMPLES OF VISION STATEMENTS

To get your creative juices flowing here are some well-known vision statements.

"Our vision is to be the world leader in transportation products and related services. We will earn our customers' enthusiasm through continuous

> *improvement driven by the integrity, teamwork,*
> *and innovation of our people."*
> **General Motors**

> *"A PC on every desktop and our software on every computer"*
> **Bill Gates, Microsoft**

> *"Our vision is to be earth's most customer-centric company; to build a place*
> *where people can come to find and discover anything they might want to buy*
> *online."*
> **Jeff Bezos, Amazon**

> *"To be the company that best understands and satisfies the product, service*
> *and self-fulfillment needs of women — globally."*
> **Avon**

CORE VALUES INFORM YOUR VISION

Before you define your vision you first need to be clear about what your core values are, as these will inform your vision.

If you're starting a business with one or more partners, then you need to make sure that you all share the core values of the company. If there's any difference of opinion on your core values, then this will cause issues in the long run.

Don't embark on a business where you have to modify your core values to suit what others expect. Doing so will create an inner conflict that will result in a negative outcome.

Your values are the things that govern how you behave, live, and work. They determine your priorities, and, deep down, they're probably the measures you use to tell if your life is turning out the way you want it to. When the things you do and the way you behave match your values, life is usually in harmony and you are satisfied and content. But when these don't align with your personal values, that's when things feel wrong. This can be a real source of unhappiness.

CORE VALUES ARE A KEY ASSET OF THE BUSINESS

Today, 80% of the Fortune 100 tout their values publicly, and companies with a high sense of purpose almost always outperform others.

Companies that effectively identify and promote their values have less employee turnover, higher customer retention, and greater profitability than those that don't.

Values exist, whether you recognize them or not. When you acknowledge your values, you can make plans and decisions that honor them.

AS THE FOUNDER, YOU SET THE CORE VALUES

One of the great advantages of starting your own business is that you, as the founder and business owner, get to set the company's values that embrace your personal core values.

You can then ensure that you hire people who are happy to share those values.

Core values are usually fairly stable, yet they don't have strict limits or boundaries. As you move through life, your values may change.

For example, when you start your career, success—measured by money and status—might be a top priority. But after you've achieved success you might decide that you're more motivated by giving back to your community.

EXAMPLES OF CORE VALUES

Zappos

Deliver WOW Through Service

Embrace and Drive Change

Create Fun and A Little Weirdness

Be Adventurous, Creative, and Open-Minded

Pursue Growth and Learning

Build Open and Honest Relationships With Communication

Build a Positive Team and Family Spirit

Do More With Less

Be Passionate and Determined

Be Humble

Adidas

Performance: Sport is the foundation for all we do and executional excellence is a core value of our Group.

Passion: Passion is at the heart of our company. We are continuously moving forward, innovating, and improving.

Integrity: We are honest, open, ethical, and fair. People trust us to adhere to our word.

Diversity: We know it takes people with different ideas, strengths, interests, and cultural backgrounds to make our company succeed. We encourage healthy debate and differences of opinion.

DEFINING YOUR CORE VALUES

Identifying and understanding your core values is a challenging and important step in building the vision for your business.

Your core values are a central part of who you are—and who you want to be. By becoming more aware of these important factors in your life, you can use them as a guide to make the best choice in any situation.

Some of life's decisions are about determining what you value most. When many options seem reasonable, it's helpful and comforting to rely on your values—and to use them as a strong guiding force to point you in the right direction.

*"It's not hard to make decisions when you know what
your values are."*

Roy Disney

KEY STEPS TO DEFINE YOUR VISION

1. Take the time to list your core values. If you can get 5 to 10 values written down, then you've begun to create the base for defining what the company stands for.
2. Take the time to define your broad vision statement. Do some competitive analysis and look at other companies' statements for inspiration. Then write a vision that fits with your core values and your goals for the business.

UNIQUE SELLING PROPOSITION

DEVELOPING YOUR USP

One of the elements that a business plan forces you to address is your Unique Selling Proposition (USP). If you're not familiar with this phrase, then you will quickly learn that this is one of the things you will get asked most about when discussing your business, i.e., what differentiates your offering from your competitors' offerings?

> *"Differentiation is one of the most important strategic and tactical activities in which companies must constantly engage. It is not discretionary."*

Thomas Levitt, Harvard Business School

Spending time defining your USP is probably the most important investment you'll make at the planning stage to ensure that your business will take off.

The more you can operate in a defined niche the more likely you can differentiate your business and the more you'll gain traction in the market.

Many new bootstrappers struggle to get their heads around this because it seems so counterintuitive.

I've worked with many business owners who try to aim for the broadest market possible. They mistakenly believe that they must appeal to as wide an audience as possible if they're going to win business.

The fallacy in this belief is that when you create a broader target market you also bring in a greater number of competitors who are all scrapping for the same bits of business.

It then becomes extremely hard to be unique in the market and the services offered become commoditized with the result that billing rates fall due to competitive pressures.

An example in a software development business would be for a company to claim that its USP is that they are "Java developers." They might even be excellent or top-quality developers but that doesn't make them in any way unique. They might think it does because they believe their competitors are rubbish and that nobody is as good as them. But the market won't know that, and it will be extremely hard to prove it. Just telling prospects how good they are will not be enough.

Think for a moment about businesses outside your area of expertise. How do you react if you see businesses advertising their USPs like these?

"Quality Dry Cleaners"

"Professional Carpet Cleaners"

"The Leading Electricians in your Area"

If you're like me, you will find these bland and meaningless propositions.

Why wouldn't any dry cleaner be a quality one?

Why wouldn't any carpet cleaner be professional?

There is nothing about these propositions that demonstrates uniqueness.

Working with the software development example from above, the company could narrow the USP by saying "We are Java developers for capital markets." This is better, as it narrows the field, but it is still too broad and doesn't make you unique.

When trying to come up with a USP the general advice is to niche down, niche down again, and then niche down again. In other words, the more you can home in on a specialist area the more valuable you are to your customers. A great USP will put you in a league of your own and will set the bar so high that only you can reach it. It will grab your audience's attention and will make them sit up and notice you.

Moving a few steps ahead, here is an example of a better USP for our Java development company:

> *"When milliseconds can be the difference between completing a deal or not then you need to be certain that you have the best high-frequency trading software experts available to you. Our Java-certified developers will ensure that your software is fully optimized to give you the maximum trading advantage possible in the open market."*

This USP has now flipped over and starts by talking about the customer's challenges.

And it's not just any customer. It's a highly specialized niche of high-frequency traders.

The USP then delivers the benefit that the customer will get by working with this company, i.e., the maximum trading advantage in the open market. This is now a much stronger USP, as it speaks directly to the target audience. It shows that the company understands the challenges the traders face and it offers the knowledge and skills that the traders will require to compete in the high-frequency trading world.

When you look at this USP you also realize that this is not a commodity service that is being offered. It is a highly specialized service with a much smaller pool of competitors. You can bet that day rates for this type of service will be much higher than standard development rates and will be much less sensitive to downward pressure from competitors.

So, the question for you is this:

Can you take your skills and knowledge and turn them into a highly focused USP like the example above?

It doesn't matter what business sector you will address or what technology you use, you should be aiming to find a niche and a value statement that positions your business as unique.

WHAT SKILLS HAVE YOU GOT?

CATALOGING YOUR SKILLS

As a first step to defining the solutions you can offer, you should first catalog all the skills that you, and any partners, have. Taking time to catalog your skills will reveal some skills that you have forgotten or overlooked or may not think are important.

In the next chapter, we will take these skills and examine how they can be used to provide solutions to customers.

CORE SKILLS

What are your core skills? As examples:

Development, testing, analysis and design, full-stack web development, front-end/GUI development, mobile app development, database administration, etc.

WHAT LANGUAGES ARE YOU SKILLED IN?

As examples:

Java, PHP, Node.js, C++, JS, C#, C, Visual Basic, ASP.NET, Knockout.js, HTML/CSS, Bootstrap, etc.

WHAT OS PLATFORMS HAVE YOU USED?

As examples:

Windows, Linux, Unix, iOS, Android, etc.

WHAT CLOUD PLATFORMS HAVE YOU USED?

As examples:

Azure, Amazon, Google, Oracle, etc.

WHAT APPLICATION PLATFORMS HAVE YOU USED?

As examples:

Salesforce, Microsoft Dynamics, SAP, SharePoint, Sitecore, Ethereum, Ripple, etc.

WHAT TOOLS ARE YOU EXPERIENCED WITH?

As examples:

Xamarin, Selenium, Jira, Git/Github, Docker, Axure, TFS, etc.

WHAT DATABASES HAVE YOU WORKED WITH?

As examples:

Microsoft SQL Server, MySQL, Oracle, SQL Azure, PostgreSQL, MongoDB, etc.

WHAT PROCESSES ARE YOU EXPERIENCED IN?

As examples:

DevOps, Project Management, Agile, Scrum, Six Sigma, etc.

WHAT SPECIALIST SKILLS DO YOU HAVE?

As examples:

Bitcoin/Blockchain, Big Data, AI, IoT, etc.

WHAT TYPES OF SYSTEMS HAVE YOU WORKED ON?

As examples:

High Availability, Trading, Mobile, eCommerce, Gaming, Knowledge Management, Blockchain, etc.

TASK TO COMPLETE

Spend some time cataloging your skillset. If you're starting a business with a partner, or partners, make sure you include all the skills you have as a group.

SOLUTIONS VERSUS SKILLS

DELIVERING SOLUTIONS

One key thing that separates seven-figure businesses from small companies and freelancers is that seven-figure businesses focus on delivering solutions whereas small companies and freelancers focus on selling their skills.

If you focus on selling skills, you will end up competing with freelancers and every other company that offers staff-augmentation services.

This will lead to a race to the bottom to see who can offer the lowest rate for the work.

You need to avoid this scenario if you are going to build a profitable, seven-figure business.

WHAT SOLUTIONS HAVE YOU BUILT?

The first step is to take your catalog of skills and then create a list of the types of business solutions you can build/deliver using those skills.

You need to think about what complete solutions customers might want from you.

A good place to start is to think back over the systems you've worked on previously. What was the solution the customer wanted?

HINT: it was NOT C#, Java development, etc.

Examples of solutions you might have worked on include retail banking, warehousing, point-of-sale, online web store, self-service, online booking, web portals, etc.

DO SOME COMPETITIVE ANALYSIS

When thinking about what solutions you can deliver do some competitive analysis. That's what all smart companies do.

Look at other software development companies, particularly the bigger ones. What solutions do they deliver?

Can you offer similar solutions or better/different solutions? Is there a specific solution area that fits well with your skills? Is there a specific solution area that interests you?

TASKS TO COMPLETE

Take the time to list the solutions you can offer.

What are the high-value solutions you could deliver?

What solutions are you most passionate about delivering?

What solution area(s) are you a real expert in?

What solutions that are in high demand can you deliver?

NICHE, NICHE, NICHE

THE FATAL MISTAKE TO AVOID

As I mentioned previously, probably the biggest mistake that most small businesses make is in trying to appeal to the broadest market possible.

I know it seems counterintuitive but when you try to appeal to everybody you end up appealing to nobody.

It becomes much harder to make yourself unique and it puts you into competition with competitors who fight at the low end of the market where price competition is rife.

Even big companies such as Apple don't try to appeal to everybody. Their devices are priced to attract a more discerning customer and that is why they are such a profitable company.

THE RICHES ARE IN THE NICHES

There's a well-known saying about competing in business

"The riches are in the niches."

The often-given advice is to niche, niche down, and then niche down again.

The more you can target a niche area the better chance you have at succeeding—as long as the niche can support your business ambitions.

WHY YOU NEED A NICHE

If you try to appeal to everybody it becomes next to impossible to know how to target your prospects. And as a small company with a limited marketing budget, you will never be able to spend enough money to attract enough profitable customers.

There are many reasons you should find a niche for your business. These include:

1) It's easier to identify and target specific prospects

2) You can more clearly vocalize your USP

3) Your marketing strategy becomes more focused

4) Your limited marketing budget can be used more effectively

5) Prospects will seek you out and pay you more

6) It's easier to become an expert and well known in your niche

7) You'll get more and better referrals

8) You'll be competing with a smaller set of competitors

PICKING A NICHE

The best niche will be a combination of a targeted solution to a targeted customer base.

Be aware that in choosing a niche you are not committing to it forever. As your company grows you will adapt to market feedback and refine your positioning.

Expansion and opportunistic events may change the niche that you will work in in the years ahead.

Start by picking the niche that fits your current skills, capabilities, and market knowledge the best.

Some questions to answer in choosing a niche include:

1) What niches have you expertise in?

2) What niche would benefit the most from your solutions?

3) What niche is most appealing to you? Could you serve it?

4) Are there enough big companies in this niche to support your aims?

5) Will customers in this niche spend enough on software development to support your aims?

TASK TO COMPLETE

Decide on a niche that best suits your skills and ambitions.

SEVEN-FIGURE CUSTOMERS

CHOOSE YOUR IDEAL CUSTOMERS

Now that you know the skills you can offer and the solutions you can deliver and the niche you can serve, your next step is to identify your ideal customers.

Remember this: It is you who chooses your customers. It is not your customers who choose you.

Choose your customers, choose your future.

By this, I mean that it should not be an accident who you end up working with. Customers will not be randomly choosing you. They will be choosing to work with you because you have specifically attracted them to your business.

If you want to build a seven-figure business, you must be clear about the types of customers you want to work with.

If you choose the right type of customer to work with then you can get to seven figures quicker and easier than if you work with the wrong type of customer.

The first thing to banish from your thinking is that you want to work with anybody and everybody. As I said previously, that approach is a big rookie mistake.

Most small businesses don't give a second thought as to who their ideal customers are. They just open their doors and hope that customers walk in.

That's why the majority of small businesses stay small and never get to seven figures and more.

My whole approach is all about landing the right type of customer so that you can profitably grow to seven figures and more.

AVOIDING BAD CUSTOMERS

A very important thing to understand is that not every customer will be a good customer for your business.

Some customers will argue about every detail of a project, every line of your proposal, every item on your invoices, and generally be a complete pain in the ass to work for.

They will stress you out and make your life miserable. These high-maintenance customers are nearly always the least-profitable customers because they soak up so much time.

Very often these types of customers will have little experience of IT projects and will have smaller budgets. These are not the type of customers that you should be aiming to work with.

IDENTIFY YOUR IDEAL CUSTOMERS

When I started my business I had some key criteria for the type of customer that we would work with. As we grew, I further refined these criteria as we figured out what worked best for us.

To help you define who the ideal customers are for your business here are the attributes that I applied to our business.

THEY WILL BE MEDIUM TO LARGE ENTERPRISES

- They will have a minimum of 100 desktops. (In reality, we usually worked with companies with 500 desktops and more and often with many thousands of desktops.)
- To get to seven figures you need to work with customers who can afford to spend significant sums on software development. You can get to seven figures with only a few of these customers.
- Small companies usually have small IT budgets. You would need hundreds of these customers to get to seven figures.

THEY INVEST HEAVILY IN TECHNOLOGY

- The more IT-driven the customer is the better. Companies that invest heavily in IT are great candidates.
- Companies that rely heavily on technology for their business to operate will be better customers for you.

THEY HAVE THE CAPACITY TO OFFER REPEAT BUSINESS

- The key to getting to seven figures is to work with customers who can offer you repeat business time and time again.
- With such customers, you have to do far less selling to get to seven figures. Repeat work usually gets offered with no competitive bidding. That's gold dust for any business.
- Small customers will only have one major IT project every few years and will rarely give you repeat work.

THEY RESPECT YOU AND NEGOTIATE FAIRLY

- You want to work with customers that respect you. Some people like to beat up suppliers. It's not worth working with this type of customer.
- The secret is to work with customers that you can build strong relationships with. If you feel that you can personally get on with the customer then that's a great place to be.
- An early sign is how they negotiate with you. If they're fair in negotiations then that's a good sign that you can build a good relationship with them. It's okay to have tough negotiations, but if it's all one-sided in favor of the customer then be wary.

BUYER PERSONAS

As well as knowing who your ideal customer is you also need to know who the people are who will buy from you. What roles do these people fulfill? What titles do they hold?

In service businesses, people buy from people. You will be dealing with these personas every time you meet with prospects, so the more you understand them the more likely you are to build rapport with them.

A buyer persona is a profile that represents your target buyer. In the software development world, there may be more than one buyer that you will deal with during the course of a sale, so knowing each persona is important.

By creating buyer personas you'll gain the ability to tailor your marketing efforts and connect with your target audience to meet their needs and solve their problems.

Also, when you know the buyer personas, and the issues they deal with in their businesses, you will be much better positioned to demonstrate your expertise and to build solid credibility in the eyes of the prospect.

TASKS TO COMPLETE

1) Write down a list of the characteristics and attributes of the ideal customers for your business. Make sure that you know who the perfect customer is for your business.

2) Write down a list of the buyer personas you will be dealing with. Who are they? What job titles do they have? What sort of decision-making responsibilities do they have? What issues are they dealing with that you can solve?

BENEFITS AND VALUE

WHAT BENEFITS DO YOU DELIVER?

By this stage, you have already defined some key aspects of your business

1) You know the services you can offer

2) You know the solutions you can deliver

3) You know the niche you can serve

4) You know who your ideal customers are

5) You know what the buyer personas are

The next key step is to define the benefits (outcomes) you deliver. This is a critical step that most small businesses overlook.

They think it's sufficient to just talk about their services and their solutions. That's a big mistake. Know this:

Your prospects don't care about you or your business.
They only care about the outcomes they get from working
with you.

Potential customers don't want to know what your solution is or does. They want to know what's in it for them. How does it make their lives better? What pains/problems does it take away?

EXAMPLES OF BENEFITS

To illustrate the concept of benefits here some examples of common products and services where the benefit is expressed:

Gloves – warm hands

Alarm clock – never be late again

Microwaves – meals in minutes

Life coach – be the best you can be

Personal trainer – ripped abs

Web hosting – sell your products online 24x7

Digital marketer – a steady stream of new enquiries

FEATURES VERSUS BENEFITS

All products and services have a set of features as well as benefits. It's important to distinguish the two from each other.

Features are facts about products or services; they add credibility and substance to your sales pitch.

Benefits give customers a reason to buy because they explain how your product or service improves their lives.

Too many salespeople focus solely on the features and neglect to talk about the benefits.

Features are important. They are the baseline things that people want or expect when they purchase something, whether that's a product or a service. They need to know that when they buy they will get their core requirements.

Features join the dots to benefits. Features act as the "evidence" for your benefits by helping you quantify the claims you're making. Without features, benefits are not as effective.

If you only focus on selling the features of your product or service, you're making the prospect do all the work to figure out why they might want the feature.

And they might even draw the wrong conclusion. It's always in your best interest to draw the connection between features and benefits for them.

THE "SO WHAT" TEST

A great way to translate features into benefits is to keep asking the "so what" question.

As an example, if you're offering Java development services here's how it would go:

We are Java certified developers.

So what?

All our developers have a minimum of eight years of Java experience.

So what?

We use SCRUM to deliver systems faster and more cost-effectively.

So what?

You will have your new system up and running within weeks rather than months so that you can generate new revenues in the shortest time possible.

With all the services that you offer you need to drill down to discover the real benefits that your customers will get. It will vary from service offering to service offering so be prepared to do this work multiple times.

If you're in a competitive situation on a deal, try and home in on the benefits that the potential prospect will get if they work with you.

Understand why they need your service and then reflect that back to them as a set of benefits by applying the "so what" test.

STORYTELLING

One of the most powerful ways to enhance your benefits is storytelling.

If you can tell a story about a similar project/situation that you worked on and explain the benefits that the customer got from your work, then you can tap into your prospects' emotional desires which is even more powerful than just talking about benefits on their own.

Make your story even stronger by talking about the transition from bad to good that you were able to make happen.

Start your story with the problems and difficulties your customer had and then explain how you were able to solve their problems with your services.

And, in case you're thinking, "I can't do this when I start my business because I have no customers," then think again.

You can tell stories from your previous experience even if the customer in question was during your time with a previous employer. Focus on the problem they had and the solution you provided.

TASKS TO COMPLETE

1) Write down a list of the features of your service(s).

2) Use the "so what" test to drive out the real benefits that prospects will get if they work with you.

3) Develop some stories about your benefits. Lean on your past experiences and turn them into bad-to-good stories that your prospects can relate to.

PRODUCTIZING YOUR SERVICES

THE SMART WAY TO SELL SERVICES

One of the best ways I know of selling services is to bundle a set of services into a "product," give it a product name, define an outcome, and set a price.

This changes the conversation about what you're offering from (time spent x rate) with no certainty as to how long it will take, to a conversation about the value of the service and the deliverables included.

Why does this work so well?

Because productizing your services makes them more tangible to customers.

It's easier for them to buy from you because they know what they are committing to and what they are getting for their money.

> *Productized services are perceived as less risky than*
> *open-ended services and are thus easier to sell.*

Productizing your services involves taking the value, skills, and advice you provide as a consultant or developer, and letting a "product" deliver part of that value.

In essence, a productized service is a value-added, systemized, "done-for-you" service, packaged neatly as a product with a defined scope and price.

In the next chapter, I'll show you why having productized services is a great way to win new customers.

CREATING PRODUCTIZED SERVICES

Start by thinking about a specific problem or requirement your ideal customer has that you can solve in a set time for a set price.

It could be a one-time fix or other deliverable or it could be a recurring service you could offer under contract. The aim is to offer a done-for-you service that a customer would be glad to buy as a product.

I recommend that you give each product a product name. It increases the credibility that it is a product. It makes it look like it's a standard thing you do.

Giving your productized service a name also reassures the customer that it's something you are an expert in. It's perceived as something that you've been able to do before.

Always use this product name when communicating both externally and internally. It's important to embed the concept of the product in everybody's mind so that they talk about it as a product.

It must always be perceived as a product in the prospect's eyes. In conversations with them, both you and they should be referring to the product rather than a set of services. This reinforces that they are buying a product with a specific outcome.

LIMIT YOUR EXPOSURE

When creating a "product" from your services you will need to be careful that you don't leave yourself open to huge cost overruns.

You must make sure that you protect your downside in case something exceeds what you intend to deliver.

You will need to be specific about what each product includes and, just as important, what it doesn't include.

You should set parameters around the inputs and outputs of your product. Manage the expectations upfront so that you don't end up with a bad outcome and an unhappy customer.

EXAMPLES OF PRODUCTIZED SERVICES

To give you some idea of how to productize services I've listed below some examples from my own company. These were different "products" we offered at various times.

Each of these products had a name, a set time, and a defined outcome. There were some parameters around some of these products to limit the exposure we had.

- Convert a Microsoft Access solution to .NET & SQL Server
- A security review of an application + recommendations
- A code review of an application + recommendations
- A performance audit of an application or database
- Building a proof-of-concept for a new technology
- Workshop/Training to transfer expert knowledge
- Service contract for a specific technology or platform

EXAMPLES OF PRODUCT NAMES

To guide you on product names here are a couple of examples from my own products.

In our early days, we had a developer support service for desktop applications such as Access & Excel. We called this DeskMan.

Later, we had an Azure proof-of-concept service that we called Azure 3-2-1. Three months, two developers and one proof-of-concept application delivered.

TASK TO COMPLETE

Take time to build a list of productized services you could offer. Define what each product consists of, the outcome it delivers and the price that you want to charge for it. Then come up with a name for the product.

UNDERSTANDING THE VALUE LADDER

WHAT IS A VALUE LADDER?

A value ladder is a way to structure your business offerings to appeal to your target audience at different points in the relationship.

It gives you a competitive edge because it ensures you have products and/or services available to continue to serve your customers as your relationship with them grows.

WHY HAVE A VALUE LADDER?

It is difficult to win a new customer with just your high-end services. It is far easier to land a new customer with a smaller, lower-cost offering.

But first, you must attract the right types of prospect and the best way to do that is to offer something for free.

The best way to attract new prospects is to offer
something valuable for free

So, the first step on the value ladder should be something valuable to your prospects that you can offer for free.

One of the best ways to do that is to offer a special research report on a topic that your ideal prospects are likely to be interested in. We'll talk more about this in a later chapter.

Step 2 on your value ladder should be a low-cost, low-risk way for the customer to evaluate you and your capabilities before deciding to use you for bigger projects.

An audit, for example, can be a fixed-price offering at a low cost. And by productizing this service you make it easier for the customer to buy from you.

The output of the audit could be a set of recommendations for the customer to implement.

Step 3 on your value ladder will be a proposition that positions your business to carry out those recommendations.

Further steps will enable you to increase your presence with the customer and to offer more valuable services to them.

THE VALUE LADDER GRAPH

Here is an example of a value ladder you could implement.

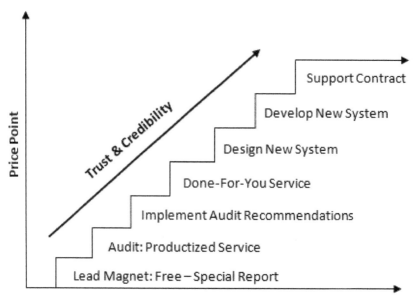

Perceived Value

The principle at play here is that it is easier to acquire new customers at the lower end of the value ladder. Then your goal is to progress the customer up through the value ladder by offering additional services as your trust and credibility grow with the customer.

Different customers can enter at different rungs of the value ladder (e.g. referrals) but you should always be looking to progress your relationship with the customer up the ladder. This is how you build a seven-figure business with relatively few customers.

For each rung of the ladder, you should have a proposition developed so that you can easily progress customers to the next step.

As you work with each customer you should be looking for additional ways that you can help them—and then put a proposition to them.

THE VALUE LADDER IS PRIVATE

The value ladder is an internal document only. It's part of your marketing approach so customers should never see it.

Customers should never feel that you are trying to progress them up a value ladder.

If they sense that your low-end offer is just designed to get you more business they may become resistant to your initial approaches.

One thing I've learned over many years is that people don't like being sold to. They prefer to buy.

That doesn't mean that you never have to sell. It just means that you must be smarter about how you get customers to buy.

One of the keys to being smarter is to have something free to give away to attract the right types of customers (I'll talk further about this in a later chapter).

This brings the prospect onto your value ladder and, when done correctly, grants you permission to have a further dialog with them and gives you the chance to progress them up the ladder.

As a customer progresses up the value ladder it should feel like a natural progression to them as you gain their trust. They will feel less like they are being sold to than they are buying more of your services. It's a very subtle but important difference.

TASK TO COMPLETE

Develop a value ladder for your solution(s). Assume that the lowest rung is a free lead magnet such as a white paper.

Make the next rung be something small that can be a fixed-price short engagement. An audit or workshop is perfect for this. Think about what done-for-you services you could offer.

What's the high-end solution you can offer and what other steps could take you there? What's the recurring product/service you can offer?

CREATING YOUR VALUE PROPOSITION

TYING EVERYTHING TOGETHER

In the previous chapters, you've been putting the pieces together that you will need to attract and win customers.

You know the services you can offer.

You know the solutions you can deliver.

You know the niche you can serve.

You know who your ideal customers are.

You know what the buyer personas are.

You know what benefits your ideal customers get.

You know what value they get from your services.

You've developed your productized services.

You've developed your value ladder.

Now it's time to create your value proposition.

A value proposition speaks directly to your ideal customers and tells them exactly why they should purchase your products or services.

A value proposition is a clear statement of the concrete results a customer will get from purchasing and using your products and/or services.

VALUE PROPOSITION FRAMEWORK

Here is a structure that can help you create your value proposition.

For _____ (your ideal customer)

who _____ (has a need or problem you can solve)

our (solution/productized service) is _____ (solution details)

that _____ (provides a clear benefit)

EXAMPLE VALUE PROPOSITION

Which of these do you think works better?

"Futures traders – we develop systems in Java to help improve your business."

versus

"Futures Traders – whenever you need new systems to enter new markets or to launch new products our TradeDesk service will provide you with high-frequency trading expertise that will have you up and trading within weeks rather than months."

This is just a simple example of how you can express a proposition in different ways.

The second version appeals to the target audience, mentions a problem they need to solve, mentions the productized service, and gives a clear benefit statement.

VALUE PROPOSITION TIPS

Do some competitive analysis to see how other similar companies express their value proposition. But beware, many small companies have poor value positions so don't model your business on theirs.

Avoid using self-promoting superlatives such as "We are the best...." This type of hyperbole turns people off. It's very hard to prove you are the best at anything, particularly in your startup days.

Avoid basing your value proposition on quality service. Why wouldn't you offer quality service? It's what buyers expect.

Saying that you offer quality service is not a differentiator on paper, but it can become a significant differentiator when you start working with a customer.

Over time you can build up some testimonials from satisfied customers that testify to your excellence and quality service. At that point, you can weave some of the comments into your value proposition.

A value proposition can also be a stack. It could be several things that together make you different.

TASKS TO COMPLETE

Develop a value proposition for each rung of your value ladder. When doing this try and see the world through your ideal customer's eyes – not yours.

What pains or problems do you solve?

What are the clear benefits you can deliver? The benefits need to be beneficial to your target audience.

What sets you apart from your competitors?

What solutions and/or productized services can you offer?

Do you offer guaranteed outcomes?

SUMMARY SO FAR

The previous chapters have all been about establishing your company and starting the process of positioning your business to win the types of customers that you want.

The preparation work you do at this stage will hugely affect your ability to succeed. This is all work that you can do before you even launch your business.

In fact, you can do all this work *before* you quit your job. This is the low-risk way to approach starting a business.

Get the groundwork done in advance and you will minimize the risks involved in launching your business.

You will also shorten the time from the launch to finding your first customer(s).

By completing these tasks, you will be well ahead of most of your competition. Even many established companies won't have done all these tasks, which is why they fail to get to seven figures and more.

In the following chapters you will learn how to take the output of this work and to use it to attract your ideal customers.

You will also complete the One-Page Business Plan.

MARKETING

THE NEW SKILL YOU NEED

You might think that being a fantastic software developer is the most important skill that you need to build a successful software development business. But you couldn't be more wrong!

Being good at software development is a prerequisite for doing your business. If you don't build top-quality software, you won't retain customers, you won't get referrals, and you ultimately won't stay in business.

But delivering great software is not enough to build and grow your business. You need to develop a new skill. A skill that will pay you back for the rest of your life.

Stack the odds in your favor by becoming a life-long student of marketing

You need to become a life-long student of marketing. If you do so, you will stack the odds in your favor, and you will massively increase your chances of building a successful business.

WHY MOST NEW BUSINESSES FAIL

Most small businesses struggle to grow and just bumble along from month to month. They will be busy for some months and quiet in other months. There will be no pattern of consistent growth.

The number one reason for this is that most people who start small businesses have never had any business training. I'm not talking about an MBA here. I'm talking about learning the fundamentals of what it takes to run and grow a business.

They think that because they're expert technicians who can do the work of the business that they will be successful.

- Plumbers start a business because they are good at plumbing.

- Electricians start a business because they are good with electricity.
- Car mechanics start a business because they are good at fixing cars.

And the same applies to most small software development companies. They are started by a developer with plenty of development experience.

But here's an irony. An experienced businessperson could probably run most of these businesses better than the expert technicians.

This is because the fundamentals of *running* a business are very different from the fundamentals of *doing* the business.

So, no matter how expert you are at software development you need to learn some other skills to be able to run a successful business.

One of the key business fundamentals that you need to learn is how to position your business so that you can consistently attract the right types of customers.

> *"The key to the success of a business is to be different in the mind of the prospect, which is what positioning is all about."*

Jack Trout

This is the crucial element that is missing in most small businesses. The business owner assumes that all they have to do is open their doors for business and customers will come knocking.

But that's not how business works and that's why most new businesses fail. They have no plan for attracting a regular stream of customers and they subsequently struggle to stay in business.

You can avoid that fate by realizing that you need some additional skills and secondly by committing to learning these new skills. That is the path to success.

When I started my business I also started reading and studying everything I could about marketing. I have invested more time and money over the years in learning everything I can about marketing.

I spent more time and money improving my marketing skills than I did in improving my development skills.

I realized that I had sufficiently good skills to *do* the business, but I needed to acquire new skills to *run* a successful and profitable business.

I strongly encourage you to adopt this mindset.

WHAT IS MARKETING?

Marketing is everything you do to attract customers to want to buy from you.

In a nutshell, marketing is the art and science of creating a need for your services or product.

Sales and marketing are often mentioned together. However, never confuse the two. They are two very different disciplines. A great salesperson might know little about marketing. A great marketer might not be a great closer of deals.

A key differentiator of the two disciplines is that, unlike sales, the goal of a marketing interaction isn't to close a sale.

The aim of marketing is to arouse curiosity and earn the right to have a conversation.

In the same way that the goal of a first date isn't to get married, the aim of marketing is to move forward, to earn attention and trust, arouse curiosity and earn the right to have a conversation.

Your ultimate goal with your marketing efforts is to get a meeting with your ideal prospect knowing that they are interested in you because of some previous interaction they've had with you.

When this is done right then the selling process is made a whole lot easier. In the perfect scenario, selling becomes a conversation between two interested parties. There is no need for aggressive sales techniques.

Isn't that something to aspire to? Wouldn't you like to engage with prospects that are interested in hearing from you and where you don't have to engage in sleazy or tricky sales techniques?

MARKETING IS NOT A SCIENCE

We know that marketing and sales are not sciences. If they were, then it would be easier to study them and know exactly what to do.

However, they're also not magical processes. There's enough case history to learn from. There are proven tactics and strategies that can help you win business.

But some work better or worse depending on the type of business you're running and your target market.

As an example, advertising on LinkedIn might be a waste of time/money if you're targeting a young audience but could be good if you're targeting a professional audience.

In the world of software development, for example, it's hard to get Google ads to work consistently for you because so many people are trying the same thing and you could be competing against hundreds or thousands of companies offering similar services.

Finding the right types of customers that will get your business to seven figures and beyond is a process that can be learned.

And once you learn that process you can apply it week after week, month after month and year after year to grow your business.

EDUCATION-BASED MARKETING

There is no single marketing tactic that is guaranteed to work with every prospect, every time. The key mantra in marketing is test, test, test.

It's all about trying different tactics, different approaches to find the best way to attract your ideal customers.

The most consistently successful way to get in front of your ideal audience that I've found is through content marketing—and education-based marketing is the strongest form of content marketing that I know of.

Education-based marketing is the sharing of your knowledge with the primary purpose of building trust. It is a strategy that builds credibility and establishes your brand as a reliable and trustworthy source of expertise.

> *Education-based marketing is the direct opposite of traditional marketing, which is done through selling-based messages.*

Most buyers in companies have had enough of traditional marketing approaches and have grown tired of hearing old and worn-out sales pitches. However, when you share valuable information and facts that help them make good buying decisions they listen.

The most effective form of education-based marketing that I've come across is The Core Story.

CORE STORY

THE LEGACY OF CHET HOLMES

The Core Story is a strategic marketing approach that was pioneered by Chet Holmes author of *The Ultimate Sales Machine.*

Chet was hailed as "America's greatest sales and marketing executive" by Warren Buffet's business partner, Charlie Munger.

Success magazine said, "Chet Holmes breaks sales records wherever he goes."

Sadly, Chet is no longer with us. He died far too young, from leukemia. Fortunately, his sales and marketing legacy lives on through his books, recorded seminars, and teachings.

A few years after starting my business, when we had a lot of cash in the bank, I brought Chet Holmes into my business along with marketing guru Jay Abraham. We invested $150,000 to learn all about the core story and how to implement it in our business. It is now my recommended method of attracting customers.

Here you will learn how to implement a Core Story strategy for a tiny fraction of what I spent to learn it.

WHY USE A CORE STORY?

Regardless of the industry you're in or the products or services you sell, more than 95% of your competitors are all selling the same way: on price, product, or service.

But if you adopt the Core Story approach you can stand out as different from your competitors.

By using an education-based approach with hard-hitting "WOW" data you can capture greater attention while simultaneously establishing yourself as an expert, authority, and educator.

This will bring more prospects in the door and will foster a level of trust and rapport that is essential to be able to turn those prospects into closed sales.

Building rapport with your prospects is probably the most important thing that you can do in any sales interaction.

However, when you try to sell, you break rapport. No one wants to be sold to.

> *Educate people to build rapport, credibility, respect,*
> *trust, and influence.*

But when you "educate," you build rapport. You build credibility, respect, trust, and influence: all key ingredients to making a sale.

A great Core Story will educate your prospects and will bring your prospects to the logical conclusion that they need to work with you before you even mention your product or service.

The Core Story approach is a very efficient way to acquire new customers by *enrolling* them rather than *selling* them. Regardless of what you sell, even if your competitors sell it at a lower price, you can dominate your market with a Core Story.

You can attract far more buyers by offering to teach them something of value than you'll ever attract by trying to sell them something.

The advantages of a great, educational Core Story include:

- Build rapport and trust that positions you strategically above your competitors
- Be positioned as an expert in the eyes of your prospects
- Dramatically upgrade the "influence" you'll have by offering solutions
- Great market data is way more impressive than a product or service and makes getting meetings easier
- Builds in a sense of urgency to dramatically reduce the sales cycle

- Establish a consistent message that can catapult your brand awareness and foster a positive and credible image

THE GOLDEN RULE

The Golden Rule for building a great core story is that you need to present compelling information that is *of value* to your ideal customers even if they have never heard about your products or services.

A great core story is loaded with bad news to your ideal customers. Why bad news? Because bad news motivates.

Your ideal customer, when viewing a great deal of bad news, will feel the need to take some action.

The data you present should "set up buying criteria" in which your product or service becomes the logical choice.

Great data can motivate your prospects in nearly all situations.

With the right core story, you can remove nearly all objections you might encounter before you even get to discuss doing business with the prospect. This is the power of a great core story.

STRUCTURE OF A CORE STORY

A great core story has a structure that takes your target audience through a bad-news narrative based on researched market data and leads them to the conclusion that you can solve their problems.

The core story structure looks like this:

1. Establish your educational based marketing and sales "core" activity founded on well-sourced market data and motivating research.

2. Ensure that the research is full of statistics, trended over time, that deliver new information to the audience creating a "WOW" through contrasting and comparing the data.

3. Information being presented is focused on the prospect - not on you. This is vital. You should not be seen to be overtly selling. You are educating.

4. The title should lead with pain. For example: "The Five Most Dangerous Trends Facing The XYZ Industry Today".

5. Content is loaded with bad news because bad news motivates.

6. The core story then becomes the "core" of all your marketing efforts: messaging, visuals, communications, web content, advertisements, social media, webinars, literature, etc.

7. Research focuses on market data rather than product data (because market data is far more motivational).

8. The data sets up the buying criteria—positioning you to gain permission to sell.

9. You help your prospects imagine a world where their problems/pain don't exist.

STEPS TO BUILD A CORE STORY

Building a core story isn't easy but becoming great at any activity isn't easy. Your commitment and dedication to building your story will pay itself back many times over and will separate you from the competition.

Research your ideal customers' industry over a 30-year period. That's where you'll find trends that no one else has spotted.

Look for the bad news. This sort of news will capture your prospects' attention and increase their motivation. When researching, specifically look for bad news that you might be able to tie to a solution that involves your product or service.

When you've gathered a body of research then you stack the info, cross-reference the info, blend it with other info, all in a delicate balance of insight that eventually leads to that prospect wanting *your* product or service over all your competitors.

CORE STORY RESEARCH

The quality of research that you do will determine the quality of the core story you end up with. You can do the research yourself, but that's not the smart way to work.

My advice is to find a researcher on www.fiverr.com and hire them to do the research. There are loads of people on there who can do the research for you very cost-effectively. They will have access to archives, databases and sources that you won't, and they'll be experienced at doing research like this.

The key to getting a good job done is to ensure that you pick somebody who can show you examples of market research they've done before. You can typically get some great research done for under $500.

Don't be cheap on this. Go for a premium provider and pay more if you have to. This research will be a foundation for all your marketing so don't try to scrimp and save on it.

> *If you produce a great core story you will recoup the costs just by winning one new customer. See it as an investment for your future.*

Before you give the go-ahead to a researcher you must ensure that you brief them so that they deliver the right type of research you need for a core story. Here are the key guidelines for the research:

Start with how their industry has developed and changed over the years. Seek out the bad news, bad trends e.g. growing competition, falling profit margins, new ways of doing business, the impact of new technologies, new regulations, etc. Find the trends that motivate buyers to buy.

What are the global pain points in the industry?

What are the costs behind these issues?

What market conditions support the need for your company?

What are the threats coming their way?

What emerging trends are surfacing that should be watched?

What local/state/country/global data and trends are happening?

What problems/failures are happening in the market?

What authorities or famous people can you quote?

Back up every piece of data with a credible source. The more you can reference external research the more credible your core story becomes. Make sure that the researcher gives you a comprehensive report. Get them to include graphs and charts and other graphics that support the research. Also, make sure you retain all copyright in the report. Once you've paid for the report it should become your property and you should be free to do with it what you want.

THE EXECUTIVE BRIEFING

Once you've got the research done the next step is to turn it into a powerful presentation that you can use to get introductions to your ideal customers.

When you talk to prospects and other people outside your business this presentation will be called an *"Executive Briefing"* rather than a presentation. Calling it an *"Executive Briefing"* carries more weight and has a sense of intrigue that will make prospects more interested in it than a standard presentation. You will reserve the phrase "core story" for internal use only.

Remember that this executive briefing is the first impression that many people will get of your business, so you need to make it a wow presentation.

Just like with the research, the smart way to work here is to hire somebody on www.fiverr.com to build a compelling presentation from the research data.

There are lots of people who can build engaging presentations with great design and powerful graphics. You just need to guide them on how you want the story to unfold based on the research you've gathered.

The presentation should be from 60 to 100 slides. Each slide should address one fact or statistic and should have an appropriate image on it.

The aim is to deliver the executive briefing in a rapid fashion in under 45 minutes. You won't dwell on any slide for a long period.

It's about serving up some hard-hitting facts that get the prospect sitting up and paying attention. Make sure that your executive briefing takes your prospect on a journey, presenting them with wow facts and statistics that show the bad news and threats facing their industry and the trends that are happening.

The briefing then leads them to the conclusion that they need to work with your company. Only at the end of the briefing do you talk about your business and how you could help them.

It's vital that there is a call-to-action (CTA) at the end of the presentation. This CTA should show them the step(s) they should take to begin working with you.

An ideal CTA, and a great way to transition them to buying mode, would be to have a productized service, e.g. an audit, that is both low-cost and easy for them to sign up to.

GENERATING ADDITIONAL CONTENT

The core story will also become the source of much of your other marketing content.

You can generate white papers, based on subsets of the research data.

You will use key data from the core story as critical content on your website.

You'll be able to use it for drip marketing campaigns and in your social media channels.

We'll talk about this in a later chapter.

CORE STORY RESOURCES

There is quite a bit of information about the core story on the internet that you can research yourself.

There are also various examples of core stories that you can check out to help you envision how yours could look.

Here is a list of resources related to the core story that I recommend. Use these to increase your understanding and appreciation of the Core Story concept.

Book: The Ultimate Sales Machine by Chet Holmes

Video: Chet Holmes – How to Become a Marketing Master
https://youtu.be/RQEH6o72BoA

Webinar: Grow Your Leads by 10X, Without Growing Your Marketing Budget with Tony Robbins and Chet Holmes
https://www.brighttalk.com/webcast/6715/34235

EXAMPLE CORE STORIES

There are a number of core story presentations in the public domain. Have a look on https://www2.slideshare.net/ for the following examples:

- Frontline Core Story https://bit.ly/2K6Xxoa
- Solutions360 Core Story https://bit.ly/37IRsGI

TASKS TO COMPLETE

1) Research the core story concept so that you understand how you can apply it to your business. Use the above resources to help you.

2) Draft a briefing document for the researcher to guide them on the industry sector you want to be researched, your ideal customers, and the type of research you want to be done.

3) Hire a researcher on an outsourcing site. Check out their previous work to ensure that they can deliver the research you need.

4) When the research is done, collate the data into a storyline that is full of wow facts and statistics and builds the bad news for the industry sector and ultimately leads to a reason why your ideal customers should work with you.

5) Hire a person on an outsourcing site to take your storyline and convert it into a compelling Executive Briefing presentation with powerful graphics. Check out their previous work to ensure that they can deliver the type of presentation you need. Don't be cheap here. Be prepared to pay a bit more for a premium presentation. Also, make sure you retain copyright in the presentation. If you are prepared to invest a few thousand dollars in getting a great story built then you could work with the research company founded by Chet Holmes, Empire Research Group http://empireresearchgroup.com/.

If any of this chapter seems daunting to you, that's okay. When you first hear about the core story you can get overwhelmed.

It's at points like this that the weak-willed and uncommitted will give up. But that's good news for you because if you stick at it you will outstrip your competitors and you will lay a platform for finding customers that will serve you for many years and will help you get to seven figures and more.

> *"Successful people do what unsuccessful people are not willing to do."*

Jim Rohn

WHITE PAPERS

WHAT IS A WHITE PAPER?

A white paper is an authoritative report or guide that informs readers concisely about a complex issue and presents the issuer's philosophy on the matter. It is meant to help readers understand an issue, solve a problem, or make a decision.

Wikipedia

White papers are another form of education-based marketing and are a staple component of a marketing strategy in most service businesses. They are a great way to establish authority in your chosen market. They build thought-leadership in an area that aligns with your products/services/solutions.

I used white papers for more than 20 years to attract prospects. In fact, I landed my first two seven-figure customers directly from white papers. Those two customers eventually spent close to $10m with us.

And to cap it all, I had the white papers written even before we officially launched our company.

COMPONENTS OF A WHITE PAPER

There are a number of components that make up a great white paper. These include:

- Rich, substantive content that educates, *not* sells
- New ideas and concepts that prompt and provoke innovative thinking
- A clearly argued position or point of view on issues that are highly relevant to your prospects
- Topical and timely content that your prospect is interested in *now*

- Statistically sound data and well-researched findings that are produced by you or that can be cross-referenced to some other authority
- A compelling title that attracts prospects to want to read the paper

WHAT MAKES A GREAT WHITE PAPER?

A great white paper is educational and even ground-breaking. Ideally, it will have your prospects nodding in agreement as they read it. As a minimum, they should be intrigued by your content.

They should come away better informed and believing that you clearly understand the challenges they are facing and that you have a solution they could use.

A well-produced white paper also establishes you as the go-to expert in your field. That not only helps justify buying from you but also paying a premium, as your company's expertise makes you a safer bet to do business with.

TIPS FOR A GREAT WHITE PAPER

Here are some tips to help you produce some great white papers.

Tip 1) Base each paper on a specific area of the core story research. Drill deeper into that area. Use stats, facts and figures, and quotable sources.

Tip 2) Know who you are writing it for. I usually have a specific person, or avatar, in mind who I know is representative of my target prospects.

Tip 3) Grab attention with a compelling title that is bad-news based. I usually use titles like

- "The seven reasons why … fail"
- "The five mistakes that …"

Tip 4) Start with an executive summary that gives a précis of the key ideas contained in the paper. These can be scanned in less than a minute by anyone, no matter how busy they are. Then they can decide whether they want to invest any more time to read the full-length document.

Tip 5) Use language your target reader is comfortable with

- Avoid technical jargon and buzzwords if the audience is non-technical
- Don't overload it with acronyms

Tip 6) Make the paper as readable as possible. The more readable it is to more likely people will read the whole paper.

- Avoid overly long paragraphs
- Use plenty of white space
- Check the readability score of the document online

Tip 7) As a guideline keep it to between 5–10 pages. That's long enough to present a solid case for your topic of expertise and short enough to be consumed easily by your prospects.

Tip 8) Use images, charts, graphs, etc., to illustrate key points, create interest, and improve readability.

WHITE PAPER RESOURCES

If you're new to the idea of white papers, one resource I can thoroughly recommend is a book by Michael Stelzner called *Writing White Papers: How to Capture Readers and Keep Them Engaged*.

This is a book that I've used as my white paper bible for many years. Do yourself a favor and order a copy from Amazon. You'll learn a lot and you won't regret it.

TASKS TO COMPLETE

Your job now is to get two to three white papers written. Use the research you've done as the foundation for the papers.

Focus on specific topics that are hot now and write papers about them.

I've always written my own white papers, as I'm comfortable writing them. It also meant that the papers were written in a style that represented me and my company.

If writing is not one of your strengths, then a site like www.fiverr.com can be your friend. There are plenty of people who will write white papers for you.

Before you hire someone, make sure that you like their writing style. Check out some of their previous papers. Very often people write in a style that will make you feel uncomfortable, so choose carefully.

At the end of the day, you have to own the white paper and stand by it. Make sure the content and tone are representative of you and your company.

Finally, make sure to retain copyright so that you can add your byline to it and you can reuse the paper and extracts in many different ways.

On completion of this stage, you should have one Core Story presentation and two to three white papers done. These will be essential elements in your marketing strategy and they can all be done *before* you launch your business.

THE DREAM 100 STRATEGY

THE DREAM 100 CONCEPT

The concept of the Dream 100 is that, regardless of the industry you're in, there is always a smaller number of better buyers than there are all buyers. In other words, not every buyer is equal. In any market, there are some buyers who are going to be better buyers than others.

Every market and every business has a subset of buyers that are their BEST buyers—meaning those who have the ability to purchase far more of your product or service, than the average buyer.

The Dream 100 is the 100 best buyers from your list of ideal customers.

The Dream 100 strategy is a way to make a consistent and constant effort to secure the business of your top 100 ideal customers.

The strategy involves building a list of 100 named ideal potential customers and just going after them relentlessly over a period spanning months.

The goal of your Dream 100 effort is to transform recognition of your business and the relationship you have with your prospects so that it goes from:

- I never heard of this company, to:
- Who's this company I've been hearing about, to:
- I think I have heard of that company, to:
- Yes, I have heard about that company, to:
- Yes, I do business with that company.

Having a Dream 100 list will enable you to target your marketing efforts and budget at the companies who could most positively affect your business.

This is the smart way to build a business when you have a limited budget to spend on customer acquisition.

The Dream strategy will also give you a significant advantage over your competitors. Most of them will never have heard of, or use, this strategy.

Knowing exactly who you want to win business from is
an extremely powerful strategy.

Get this right and you lay a platform for consistently winning new customers.

DREAM 100 CAMPAIGN

An effective Dream 100 campaign is a coordinated effort that utilizes a variety of strategic elements that will enable you to establish rapport, brand awareness, market education, need and potential pain that impacts your ideal buyers.

This initial Dream 100 campaign is designed to last at least six months in order to maintain "Top of Mind" awareness and persistence to get the target to commit to action.

Over a period of six months, you will continue to target your Dream 100 with a series of activities. Every few weeks you will send them a letter with a lumpy gift. You will follow up with a call. Your goal is to get the opportunity to present your executive briefing.

The Dream 100 Strategy is the fastest, easiest way to build any company. But you need to have the discipline and persistence to follow through. You must have a dogged determination to make this strategy succeed.

THE DREAM 100 LUMPY LETTER

The principle of this approach is that you send them a letter with a lumpy gift in it. This approach pretty much guarantees that it will get attention and ultimately increase recognition. The gifts must be inexpensive tchotchkes. You must not appear to be trying to bribe them or buy business from them. You can buy them online for cents. You can use a site like www.alibaba.com to buy them in bulk.

The letter will reference a key point in your core story. The tchotchke will relate to your headline.

As an example, a measuring tape could have a tagline such as

> *"How do you measure up in your use of Scrum? 93% of companies like yours are doing it wrong and it's costing them millions of dollars every year".*

In the letter, you will refer to the executive briefing that you sponsored. You could correctly claim that there is more than $x million dollars of research involved in the report. This is because the various companies that you cite in your executive briefing will have spent substantial sums doing their research.

DREAM 100 FOLLOW-UP CALL

In the days following your mailing campaign, you will follow up each letter with a call to the person you've mailed.

You will cross-reference your letter and talk about your executive briefing.

Your goal is to get them to invite you in to present your executive briefing. Explain that it takes less than 45 minutes. Give them a synopsis of some of the key points you'll address, making sure that those points are hot topics in your market.

One tactic you can use to counter any resistance is to frame the briefing as an educational session that you'd be happy to deliver in a lunch-and-learn session.

MAKING THE STRATEGY WORK

Much of what I've written about the Dream 100 strategy is almost certainly outside your comfort zone. That's okay. I don't expect that you knew any of this stuff. The key is not to let it stop you from achieving your goals. There is nothing particularly difficult about it. The main attributes needed are a desire to succeed and a persistence and commitment to sticking at it.

You must be prepared to stretch yourself if you want to
build a seven-figure business

If you're going to build a seven-figure business, you're going to have to stretch yourself. I had to push myself in the early days of my business and learn new skills and take on tasks that I thought I couldn't do. But it paid off.

This is the stuff that separates entrepreneurs from wannapreneurs. If you step up and crack this, you will put yourself FAR ahead of your competitors because they will never have heard of this strategy.

You should be able to see that this approach will beat advertising for work on Craigslist, Odesk, etc., hands down.

Using the Dream 100 strategy enables you to build a position of authority with your ideal customers. This will reduce price sensitivity and will help you avoid having to compete on price.

And never forget this: You only need to land one of your Dream 100 prospects and your business could explode.

DREAM 100 EXECUTION TIPS

To keep costs down you can do all the letters and posting yourself. I spent many evenings with my wife stuffing letters and tchotchkes into envelopes.

If you, or your partner(s), are not comfortable at making calls, then you could use an outsourcing site to hire a salesperson to make the calls. A good salesperson could significantly improve your chances of getting appointments with your Dream 100 prospects. Make sure that they know your core story and follow the structure. They are not trying to sell anything. They are only trying to get you an appointment.

Pay people based on the number of briefings they get you. I would also advise that you listen to some of their calls so that you're comfortable with how they represent you and your business. Having one person do the call, and a different person present the briefing, can subtly indicate that you are a sizeable company.

TASKS TO COMPLETE

Begin the process of building your Dream 100 target list. The list could be more than 100 companies but aim for a minimum of 50.

You will only need to get one or two of these as a customer and your business could take off.

Use your buyer persona as a guide to establish who the potential buyers of your services are.

The obvious place to start building your list is LinkedIn. All your prospects will likely be on LinkedIn.

There are other sites that can help you build your Dream 100 list. In the U.S. you can use a site like http://www.hoovers.com/ to research your prospects.

If you need help researching the list then you can use an outsourcing site to get somebody to help you.

These researchers typically have access to databases that you wouldn't have. These databases will often have full contact details such as email address phone number etc.

Plan out your campaign letters and buy the tchotchkes for each letter.

If you plan to use somebody else to do the follow-up calls, then find a salesperson and brief them on your story.

Send out your first letter to your Dream 100 list.

Make the initial follow-up calls.

Repeat on a regular cycle.

YOUR FIRST CUSTOMERS

LANDING NEW CUSTOMERS

Landing your first customer is the initial step in validating your business idea. It builds confidence that you can go on to grow your business. It also starts generating revenue and, all going right, enables you to get your first references/testimonials.

There is no single way that is guaranteed to land you your first customer(s). There are multiple tactics you can try. At least one of them is likely to pay off. The key is to get out there in your market and put your name about in a structured way.

> *Hustle is the name of the game when you're growing a*
> *new business. You can't afford to be shy at this stage.*

The most important thing in finding customers is your mindset. You need to realize that every place you go is a chance to find customers and act accordingly. You don't need to be pushy or obnoxious, just be friendly, open, and aware when you are presented with an opportunity. Remember that the best salesman for your business is *you*. Be prepared to get out of your comfort zone and be prepared to spend some money. Don't be cheap.

Now let's look at how to land your first customer.

YOUR CURRENT EMPLOYER

Many people will be surprised by this, but your current employer could be your best bet to become your first customer.

If you're an important cog in the wheel at your employer and/or you have specialist skills or knowledge that they would like to keep, then your chances of doing a deal with your employer could be very good.

As an employer myself I never wanted to lose my key people. If a key person was about to leave but offered to continue working for me through their own company I would often jump at it. I've hired a number of people this way.

If you have a good relationship, and a good reputation, with your employer, then try it. Just ask! You might be surprised at how easy it is to do a deal.

If you do get a chance to do a deal with your current employer then I have a few words of caution.

Before agreeing on a deal, you must ensure that you stack some things in your favor.

1) You must agree on a commercial rate. This must be more than the salary equivalent. It should be a rate that generates profit into your business so that you use those profits to grow the business.

2) You must agree that you can use other people on the job. If you don't do this then you will lock yourself in and won't be able to grow your company. If you get locked in then you are effectively becoming a freelancer. You can't build a seven-figure business that way. You might not have anybody else you can use at the beginning, but your aim should be to bring other people on board and for them to replace you so that you can focus on building the business.

A CURRENT CUSTOMER

You might already work for a company that delivers software development services. Every company has some customers they would be happy to lose so you might be able to pick up a customer from your employer. Just ask.

Alternatively, your employer might have a customer where you're critical to the relationship they have. If they lost you they might also lose the relationship with the customer. You might be able to negotiate a way to work with the customer that works for both you and your employer.

This would be a way to build credibility and generate revenue quickly.

YOUR EMPLOYER'S CUSTOMERS/CONTACTS

Your employer may be prepared to refer you to some of their current customers/contacts. Such a referral is worth its weight in gold. This would work particularly well when you're not competing with your employer.

A PAST CUSTOMER OF YOUR EMPLOYER

You might have worked at a past customer of your employer, but they are no longer an active customer for them. As long as you don't breach any contractual restrictions you should contact them and tell them about your business.

A PAST EMPLOYER

If you have good relationships with any of your past employers, then contact each one of them and tell them about your business. Offer to take them to lunch to update them. Use that lunch to tap them for opportunities they might have to use your company.

By paying for the lunch you can bring in the law of reciprocity, i.e., they may feel that they owe it to you to help you out.

A PAST EMPLOYER'S CUSTOMERS/CONTACTS

If you have good relationships with past employers, then when you meet or contact them to talk about your business ask about their customers and their contacts. Get names, job titles and contact numbers. Have you worked with any of their customers in the past? Could you contact them directly yourself? Could they give you a testimonial that you can use when talking to their customers or contacts?

FAMILY

Tap into *all* of your family networks and tell them about your business. Even cousins or distant relatives might have valuable contacts you should talk to. Ask them specifically if they know anybody who you should talk to. Get names, job titles, and contact numbers. Also, ask them for a contact name at their current company.

One tip I'd give is that you're better off not relying on other people to tell their contacts about your business. It's far better if you get their name and you then contact them yourself. You can explain your business much better than anybody else can.

FRIENDS

Meet with *all* your friends and tell them about your business. Ask them specifically, do they know anybody who you should talk to. That could be somebody at their current company, somebody they've worked with before, or somebody they know in their network. Get names, job titles and contact numbers.

FORMER COLLEAGUES

Contact former colleagues. Find out where they're working and where they've worked previously.

Ask them specifically, do they know anybody who you should talk to. Is there anybody at their current company you could talk to? Get names, job titles and contact numbers.

LINKEDIN CONTACTS

Tap into your LinkedIn network. You do have one, don't you? Let them know that you've set up a business. Craft a message around your business and core story. Reach out to these contacts. Have a beer/coffee/lunch with them. Get names and contact details of people they could introduce to you.

Check your contacts to see if they are connected with anybody on your Dream 100 list. Get them to refer you or introduce you. Offer to buy dinner/lunch if it gets you a meeting with them.

LINKEDIN GROUPS

Find out what groups your Dream 100 people are active in. Join those groups and start contributing where you can. Reply to, or comment on, one or more of their posts. Engage with them and build credibility but don't pitch for work at this stage. Get recognized first for your expertise. Then you could approach them about presenting your core story.

NETWORK IN YOUR COMMUNITY

Go to local meetups or events that might have some of your ideal customers, or even their suppliers, there.

You might meet suppliers or customers of your ideal customers. They might be able to refer you or give you a contact name.

This next tip may seem counter-intuitive, but it's essentially like establishing enough karma that will pay off in the near future.

Instead of focusing on what you can get from your network, spend time focusing on what you can give.

Can you offer to do a presentation around your core story or one of your white papers?

Here are some additional tips about networking.

1) Be prepared to answer the question "So, what do you do?" over and over and over again. This is your elevator pitch. Refine it and practice it until you can succinctly explain it to people.

2) Wow people with your awesomeness. People buy from people they like, so be enthusiastic and knowledgeable. Smile.

3) Leave them with business cards so they can internet stalk you when they get home.

4) Follow up promptly with people you meet especially if you promised to send them something (e.g. a white paper).

ATTEND INDUSTRY EVENTS

Identify the key industry events in your market and plan to attend at least one of them. Usually, there are one or two major events annually. You can often attend an event as a visitor without access to the sessions. It's cheaper that way.

Go with a purpose to meet key targets of yours. Have a list of those people with you and seek them out. A great way to approach people is to tell them you're doing a survey. The more that this survey relates to your core story the better.

Ask them if they could answer, say, five questions for you. Go with a clipboard and form to make it look realistic. Exchange business cards and promise to send them the results of the survey.

You could spice things up and enter them in a draw for a prize. Then, some days later, send them some branded merchandise as a prize winner. Both approaches will help them remember you and make it easier to have a follow-up call with them.

SPEAK AT INDUSTRY EVENTS

Getting the opportunity to speak at an industry event would put you center-stage in front of your ideal customers. Don't present your full core story. Reserve that for direct meetings with a prospect. You could present a synopsis and invite attendees to contact you afterward to arrange for a full presentation.

Alternatively, present one of your white papers focused on a specific problem area. Make sure you get people signed up to receive your other papers/content. You can do this by offering to email your slide presentation to people.

LOCAL COMPETITORS

Collaborating with your competitors is another step that may seem counterintuitive, but you would be surprised how many companies will subcontract services. Many companies land big projects that stretch their resources and they often need additional help to fulfill the project.

> *Your competitors could be a great source of work for you.*

If you know of competitors in your market, then go and have lunch with them and see if they get overloaded and need additional help. This is something that I frequently did, and we regularly partnered with companies that we might otherwise have seen as competitors.

When meeting with competitors make sure that you meet on a peer basis whenever possible, i.e., founder to founder.

Build a relationship at the top level, as it's vitally important that you work with people you feel you can trust and who won't require you to operate in conflict with your core values.

NON-LOCAL COMPETITORS

Similar to local competitors, if you know of any non-local companies working in your area, then go and meet them and offer them local assistance. Many non-local companies would be happy to have a local partner on the ground and in the same time zone.

COMPLEMENTARY PROVIDERS

There are always people/businesses that are complementary to yours. They could be targeting the same customer base, or they might work with one or more of your ideal customers. An example could be a graphics designer or website designer. They may have lots of front-end skills but no back-end skills. Together you could offer a more valuable service to customers.

Another example is a consultancy that helps advise companies but doesn't have any development capability. Working together you could offer a better service.

Over the years we worked with many complementary providers, particularly consultancies, and it was generally a win-win-win situation, i.e., we won more business, they won more business, and the customer got a better job done.

Don't be afraid to put yourself about and talk to these companies. If you have a valuable skillset that these other providers can use, then this can prove to be a good source of new business.

OUTSOURCING SITES

In general, I don't recommend using outsourcing sites such as Elance, Upwork, Craiglist, oDesk, Freelancer, etc., to find work. You're bidding mostly on price and you're competing with overseas people with low costs and low rates. That's not a sustainable way to grow a business.

However, if it gets you some early credibility and a testimonial from an ideal customer, then it could help. Choose a good project that acts as proof of your capabilities. But don't get stuck here. It's hard to stand out. and it's hard to make good margins and you're very unlikely to get to seven figures. Make sure that you carry on with all your other customer attraction activities.

TIPS TO WIN YOUR FIRST CUSTOMERS

Never be desperate for work. Desperation is like radiation. It will leak out from all your pores. Prospects will never choose you if you're desperate. Exude the confidence of a successful businessman and you will attract people to you. Prospects like to work with successful businesses.

Always appear to be busy and in demand. If they ask about your availability don't immediately suggest a date. Check your calendar and "move things around to fit them in."

TASK TO COMPLETE

Simple. Go find your first customer(s).

SALES

SALES VERSUS MARKETING

Sales and marketing are two quite different disciplines although they are often mentioned in the same sentence.

I would explain the difference between sales and marketing like this:

Marketing is the art and science of creating a need.

Sales is the process of converting interested prospects into paying customers.

This quote gives a good explanation of what sales is

"I like to think of sales as the ability to gracefully persuade, not manipulate, a person or persons into a win-win situation."

Bo Bennett

A key phrase in this definition is *"gracefully persuade, not manipulate."* In other words, you don't have to tell lies or be sleazy to be good at sales. Quite the contrary.

I've personally found selling to be relatively easy by being open and honest. I've encountered plenty of people who try to be tricky or sleazy, but they never last in business. They eventually get found out.

YOU CAN DEVELOP SALES SKILLS

I know from my own experience that sales is probably the area of least comfort for most software developers. I also know that many developers look down on salespeople and regard them as shifty types.

However, that lack of comfort with sales usually occurs because developers, like most employees, have had little exposure to the sales process in their company. Most employees have no real idea of how their employer wins new business because they don't operate on the front line. Most developers work in the back office of their employer and are often shielded from the sales and marketing activities.

The good news for you is that if you follow the processes in this book, you won't have to do anything sleazy, tricky, or manipulative to become good at selling.

YOU ARE THE BIGGEST ASSET

The best salesperson for your business is *you*.

Being a founder gives you extra credibility over an employee. A title, such as CEO or president, further enhances your credibility when you are talking to other decision-makers. Prospects react well to passion, so your passion for your business is a key selling point.

> *Your status as the business owner gives you added credibility*

There will be times where prospects or customers will only want to deal with you as the business owner. They will want to feel comfortable working with your company, so they will want to meet with you. It follows, then, that selling is a valuable skill for you to develop as you grow your business.

I can tell you that some of the most exciting days I've had in business were when we signed big deals with a new customer. That's the type of buzz you don't get from programming. If you can learn to love both marketing and selling then you will set yourself up for success.

PEOPLE BUY FROM PEOPLE

Success in sales is primarily about building rapport with your prospect.

When you build rapport with your prospects you develop mutual trust, friendship, and affinity with them. If you can establish good interpersonal relationships many doors will open for you.

Here are some guidelines for handling sales situations and building rapport:

1. Be yourself; don't attempt to be clever or obsequious

2. Smile and engage with them in a friendly and open manner

3. Listen more than you speak. Avoid interrupting the prospect because that is one sure way to break rapport

4. Ask questions based on what you've heard. This is a great way of showing the prospect that you are listening to them

5. Always have a can-do attitude; prospects hate people who make things difficult

6. Learn to recognize the different character types and adapt to them.

It's worth spending some time learning how to establish rapport with prospects. It's a skill that will pay you back throughout your career.

Here's a video I recommend you check out:

Six Scientifically Proven Steps to Building Rapport with Anyone in Sales

https://youtu.be/8K-BtYu7n28

SALES MEETING TIPS

Your ultimate goal with all your marketing efforts is to gain interest from your Dream 100 prospects and then to be able to convert that interest into getting a meeting with them.

Sales meetings are the most important outcome you can achieve from your marketing, so make sure that you prepare for them and that you put your best foot forward. Never forget that a successful sales meeting can lead to big success for your business.

Here are my tips, based on the experience I gathered in more than 25 years of attending sales meetings.

ALWAYS BE ON TIME

Never, never, never be late for a meeting. Be 30 minutes early rather than two minutes late. Ten minutes early is perfect etiquette. You've worked your butt off to get the meeting. Don't blow it by falling down on basic stuff like timekeeping.

Being late communicates a lot, and none of it is good.

DRESS THE PART

You are being visually and mentally judged the moment you come within sight of a potential customer. Their perception of your competence starts then. Make sure your dress and grooming don't give off the wrong impression. Remember, you've chosen them as a potential customer so make sure that you go ready to win their business. There is no single recommended dress code because it will depend on the type of company you're going to meet and the environment you're meeting in.

If you're meeting a legal firm or a bank, say, in swanky downtown offices then you can probably bet that everybody will be wearing suits. So, you should probably be more formally dressed.

If you're meeting a hip media firm, then the likelihood is that they all dress casually so you could relax your dress code. But avoid going too far with torn jeans, T-shirts, etc.

> *It's hardly ever wrong to look dressed up in a*
> *business meeting.*

If you're in any doubt about how to dress, then lean to the formal side. A suit or jacket and shirt/blouse is rarely the wrong choice and it shows a level of professionalism and care about your job.

HAVE A GOOD HANDSHAKE

The first physical contact you have with a prospect is usually a handshake. It's one of the early things that will help a prospect decide if they like you. Various studies have shown that a handshake can improve the quality of an interaction, producing a higher degree of intimacy and trust within a matter of seconds. Management experts at the University of Iowa declared handshakes "more important than agreeableness, conscientiousness, or emotional stability."

Conversely, a bad handshake can instantly lose rapport and trust with the prospect even before you sit down to talk to them. The worst type of handshake is what I call the dead fish handshake. This is the limp, lifeless hand extended and just barely shaken. This is guaranteed to put people off.

Make sure you meet their handshake. Be firm but not too firm. Don't try a knuckle crunching handshake especially if you're meeting a female prospect.

GO PREPARED

It's amazing how many people go to a sales meeting without doing any advance preparation. Don't be one of them.

Find out all you can about your prospect in advance. Check out their website and learn about their business. Always know how they make money.

Google them to see if there were any recent press releases. You can use this information during your meeting to show that you know something about their business.

Check LinkedIn to see if you share any contacts. Use that knowledge in the meeting. If you share a contact, then call the contact to see what information they can give you about your prospect. Is the person you're meeting on social media? What interests do they have? Do you share interests?

Knowing more about your prospect and their business in advance empowers you to build empathy and rapport.

DON'T BE TOO FAMILIAR TOO SOON

Becoming familiar too soon is a classic stereotype of a pushy, insincere, salesperson. You don't want to be one of those. It's always better to err on the side of formality with people's names.

When you meet people named Michael and Nicole, don't initially assume that you can call them Mike and Nicky. If you hear them call each other those less formal versions of their names, you may ask their permission to use them.

PUT YOUR PHONE ON SILENT

Never, ever have your phone go off in a meeting. That's guaranteed to break rapport and will most likely lose you any chance of working with the prospect.

If by mistake your phone does go off because you forgot to put it on silent then whatever you do don't answer it. That is just a big no-no. You can usually recover the situation by apologizing and saying "Sorry, I thought I had put it on silent." Then make a visible move to put it on silent so that the prospect knows it won't happen again.

LISTEN MORE THAN YOU TALK

Adopt the approach that you have nothing to sell until you know what the prospect's problem is. Then pay attention to the prospect's needs from the start and respond accordingly.

> *Listening carefully and asking intelligent questions are*
> *great ways to build rapport.*

Learn to ask intelligent questions that reveal your knowledge of the topic. There is no such thing as a "natural-born salesperson." Anyone can learn to be good at sales, including you!

TAKE NOTES

Taking notes makes you look professional. It shows the prospect that you're interested and paying attention. I recommend investing in some quality Black 'n' Red notebooks. Notes help you recap during the meeting and they also help you remember the follow-up actions after the meeting.

PAY ATTENTION TO YOUR BODY LANGUAGE

Your body language is another attribute that will be instantly judged by the prospect. Looking at your phone or your watch, playing with your pen, touching your hair, looking out the window, etc., are all distractions that you need to avoid during the meeting. These behaviors can make your buyer feel like you're either in a rush to be elsewhere or that you're bored.

Your goal is to make the prospect feel important so make sure that you make plenty of eye contact with them.

Nodding occasionally to show your understanding or agreement with them is another powerful behavior that helps build rapport.

Tilting your head slightly when you are listening to someone speak communicates that you are giving them your undivided attention.

These are simple little behaviors that can work in your favor, as long as you pay attention to them.

NEVER DUCK AN OBJECTION

In any sales meeting, you are likely to get some objections. Skilled buyers will often throw these out just to see how you react. Don't get put off by these objections. Objections are often buying signals. An un-resolved objection will always remain an objection, so never leave an objection hanging. Clarify the objection if you need to but never dismiss it. Pause and answer thoughtfully. Respect their point of view while giving your answer.

Pivot the objection into an advantage if you can. For example, an objection that you might hear is "We think you're too small for us to work with." You can pivot the objection by saying something like "Sure, we're not as big as an Accenture but we're more highly focused on your industry and we can give a more personal service."

NEVER GUESS AT AN ANSWER

Prospects will often ask you tough questions, and you may not always know the answer. The person asking you may be testing you. They quite likely will know the answer themselves, but they want to test your knowledge and see how you handle it. Don't guess if you don't know the answer. If you waffle or give a poor answer, it's very hard to rebuild credibility. It's okay to say that you don't know but that you could get the answer for them.

DON'T BE OBSEQUIOUS OR FAWNING

The more you can agree with what your prospect is saying the easier you can build rapport. Up to a point! You don't have to agree with everything the prospect says. It's okay to respectfully disagree at times. In fact, this can increase your credibility if you handle it respectfully and politely. If you can use a story of a previous case study to show why you disagree then that can really help your credibility.

NEVER BE MODEST ABOUT YOUR PRICES

If you get talking about prices in a meeting never be afraid to say confidently what your prices or rates are. The more confidently you can talk about your rates or prices without squirming or apologizing the more likely you will get the rate or price you want.

> *Build value first before you talk about price but then be*
> *confident in your prices.*

If you give any hint that your price is negotiable, tentative, or even in the wrong ballpark, then this will suggest to the prospect that it may be aspirational and that you don't believe in it. And if you don't believe in it then why should your prospect believe in it?

KNOW WHEN TO STOP SELLING

One of the greatest failings in many so-called "professional salespeople" is their compulsion to talk too much. There are certain times when it is important to stop selling. The most important time is when you make a sale. Once you close the sale then you must stop selling. Carrying on selling at that point can only do damage and may lose you a sale that is already in the bag.

Too many salespeople carry on selling after making the sale and start undoing all their good work. Don't make this rookie mistake. Rather than carrying on selling, shift into discussing the details of getting the deal closed, delivered, implemented, etc. Even discussing the weather can be better than trying to keep selling!

KEEP LEARNING ABOUT YOUR CUSTOMERS

Every time you're with a prospect or customer, make it a point to learn something personal and professional about them. Learn about their family and their hobbies. Look for areas of common interest to you both. Build rapport around these areas.

Have they got kids? How many? Boys/girls? Names?

What sports or hobbies are they interested in?

Do they get to travel a lot? What are their favorite destinations?

What types of food do they like to eat?

Obviously, you don't blurt out all these questions in one go or at one meeting. You gradually pick up this information through casual conversations with them.

These are the things that will help you propel the business relationship to the next level and help you retain customers for the long term. Keep notes of this information (in a CRM system) and replay things back to them at a later date.

For instance, if you learned that your customer's son or daughter was about to take an important exam, then the next time you meet the customer you could casually ask how their son/daughter fared in the exam.

IN SUMMARY

The main point of these tips is that when trying to win business every little nuance counts. Stack the odds in your favor by paying attention to these tips. Make sure your staff also follow your lead. Anybody likely to engage with a customer or prospect should be coached on these tips.

CHOOSING A SALES METHODOLOGY

WHAT IS A SALES METHODOLOGY?

You might be surprised to discover that many professional services companies don't just sell randomly. Most successful companies will operate within a structured sales methodology.

A sales methodology enables you to have a more structured and strategic approach to bring deals to closure.

If you're coming from a non-sales background, then adopting a sales methodology will improve your chances of closing more deals. It will help you understand the steps involved in closing complex software development deals.

There are tens of thousands of books on sales and there are hundreds of sales methods and frameworks. So which methodology should you choose?

MILLER HEIMAN

One framework that I like and that fits the type of sales that you will be engaging in is Miller Heiman – Strategic Selling with Perspective.

This is a proven framework to make sure you will do a thorough job of covering a given account. It is particularly relevant to complex sales such as software development sales. By complex, I mean that the buying organization has many options. There are usually at least several people on the buying side, and they are evaluating many options including "do it yourself."

The core of the Miller Heiman approach involves:

1. Categorizing the different contacts/roles by their influence on the sales cycle.

2. Then determining their level of support for your proposition to flag the ones that would oppose it or go with it.

3. Working those people to help them reach a consensus for a buy decision.

The four key roles to identify in a complex sale are:

1. Decision-makers/economic buyers: The people who will sign the order. You need to win their support to get the deal approved.

2. Technical buyers: The people who have to say that your proposition is delivering on the promise and meets the company requirements (IT, purchasing, legal, etc.).

3. User buyers: The people who will be affected by your proposition.

4. Champion: The person who wants to make you win and give you insider info on the account.

Each role could be one or more individuals. In some situations, one person will fulfill more than one of these roles.

SALES METHODOLOGY RESOURCES

It's vital that you understand some of these nuances of selling if you want to win large deals.

If you're going to get to seven figures and more, you will find yourself in situations where having a sales methodology will help you navigate the complexities of the deal.

It's worth investing time in understanding more about this topic. As a starting point, I recommend you have a read of this book about

Miller Heiman: *The New Strategic Selling: The Unique Sales System Proven Successful by the World's Best Companies*

You can also watch a series of videos about the Miller Heiman methodology here

https://www.youtube.com/watch?v=diShJG1XX8c

THE ART OF SELLING

HOW TO SELL

Sales should never be about using hard-nosed tactics. First and foremost, it's about building rapport and developing relationships.

Put your prospects' needs first and you will start to build trust and rapport. This will eventually lead to long-term success.

When you encounter a great salesperson, you don't even realize you are being sold to. They don't come on to you in a loud and blatantly obvious manner like the traditional used-car guy.

Great salespeople have normal conversations with prospects and help them make a good decision.

It is a discovery process for both parties, not just a sales presentation.

When done right, selling is an honest conversation about whether there is a good fit, followed by a decision to move forward or part ways.

BUILDING RAPPORT

I previously discussed rapport and how important it is to the selling process. Here are some further tips on building rapport.

MATCH THEIR COMMUNICATION STYLE

One of the best ways to build rapport is to match the prospect's communication style.

If you're with a direct person, be direct. If you're with a fun, outgoing person, be more fun and outgoing. If you're with a very introverted, detailed person, act more subdued and present concise, accurate information. The key to real rapport is treating other people the way they wish to be treated.

BE GENUINE AND BE YOURSELF

Don't try to be anything you're not. Don't try to create a new persona or adopt a "sales-like" tone.

Relax, smile, and go in with a positive attitude. Good things will follow.

> *"Be yourself; everyone else is already taken."*
> **Oscar Wilde**

GIVE GENUINE COMPLIMENTS

Sycophants get nowhere, but genuine compliments are endearing.

If you like the prospect's office, their web site, or are impressed with something else, say so. If your prospect had a recent accomplishment then relay your authentic congratulations. Doing these things can go a long way toward building rapport—and they'll appreciate it.

USE HUMOR APPROPRIATELY

Sharing a laugh is a great way to build rapport but be careful because not all people want to be light-hearted in a meeting. Save your jokes until you've developed the relationship.

SHOW INTEREST

The more genuinely interested you appear to be in them, the more relaxed and willing to share they're likely to be. And they will become more interested in you.

> *"To be interesting, be interested."*
> **Dale Carnegie, How to Win Friends and Influence People**

KNOW YOUR CORE STORY BACK TO FRONT

Know the facts and figures contained in your core story and use these appropriately in your conversation. Engage the prospect around some of these areas. This will build your credibility.

QUALIFYING A SALES OPPORTUNITY

Not all sales opportunities that you'll get will be good ones. Qualifying is all about gathering insights necessary to make a good judgment on how you should proceed with an opportunity, or not.

- Should you sell to a given prospect?
- What is the best course of action to close a deal?
- Is this prospect a good fit for your offer?
- Is it a viable sales opportunity?
- Are you talking to the right people?
- Do they have the authority and budget to buy?

If you're not qualifying your leads properly, you'll waste a lot of time following up, and attempting to sell to prospects that aren't a good fit for your business. It's far better to spend this time on qualified prospects because you'll close substantially more valuable deals.

Use the BANT framework as a starting point for qualifying an opportunity. Originally developed by IBM, BANT covers all the broad strokes of opportunity and stakeholder-level qualification.

BANT seeks to uncover the following four pieces of information:

- Budget: Is the prospect capable of buying?
- Authority: Does your contact have adequate authority to sign off on a purchase?
- Need: Does the prospect have a business pain you can solve?
- Timeline: When is the prospect planning to buy?

TENACITY IN SELLING

Tenacity is the most valuable trait you can have when selling. Herbert True, a marketing specialist at Notre Dame University, found that:

- 44% of all salespeople quit trying after the first call
- 24% quit after the second call
- 14% quit after the third call
- 12% quit trying to sell their prospect after the fourth call

If you work it out, this means that 94% of all salespeople have quit after the fourth call. But here's the killer point. Statistics show that of all sales made, 60% of them are made after the fourth call. So, if you stop trying after being told No four times then you're taking 60% of your potential sales off the table.

Can you afford 60% fewer sales?

So how can you break the mold? Simple. Go back at least five times to a prospect. And when you go back the fifth time think to yourself "60% of the time, it works every time."

DISCIPLINE IN SELLING

If you crave the financial and personal freedom that a successful business can provide, you must be willing to go the extra mile. If that means working on a Friday night when all your friends are at happy hour, then so be it. If that means getting up hours earlier each morning until you master your new skills, then that's what you must do.

The sacrifices you make today will pale in comparison to the reward you'll enjoy later.

Here are a set of disciplines you should abide by

- Make those calls; always stay active in sales
- Do those things you don't want to do
- Return calls to prospects/customers as soon as possible

- Record your interactions with prospects/customers in a CRM system
- Be constantly studying and learning about sales

RISK REVERSAL

YOUR SECRET WEAPON

Risk reversal is one of the most powerful, and least known, sales techniques available to you.

This is a technique I learned from the great Jay Abraham. He has helped thousands of businesses grow exponentially using this technique.

Very few businesses know what risk reversal is or how to use it.

If you implement risk reversal in your business, it will be your secret weapon for winning new business.

When I implemented risk reversal in my company it helped me make sales that I might not otherwise have won. It is especially important when trying to land a new customer.

WHAT IS RISK REVERSAL?

When two parties come together to transact business, one side is always asking the other to assume most or all of the risk. That's a simple fact of business.

The problem is, when the person who must assume the risk is your prospective customer, the natural inclination is to hesitate, to be suspicious and uncertain and ultimately to not buy. What makes them hesitate?

They're concerned that once they've paid you their hard-earned money, your product or your service will not meet their expectations.

They may also be afraid of looking foolish or being embarrassed if the purchase doesn't turn out right or is an astute buy.

In the end, your prospect's decision whether or not to buy from you will be motivated by two things:

- their confidence in your product or service

  and

- the level of risk (consciously or unconsciously, explicitly or implicitly) you're asking them to shoulder in the transaction.

These two factors are often inversely related. If you can lower the level of risk for the buyer you can increase the level of confidence they have.

USING RISK REVERSAL TO MAKE SALES

Your challenge is to figure out the best way you can reduce or eliminate the element of risk or fear on the part of the buyer.

Reduce, or take away, the risk and you lower the barrier to action. You make it much easier for them to say Yes.

And if your value proposition carries less risk than your competitors', prospects will not only be more inclined to say Yes, they'll be much more likely to buy from you rather than a competitor.

RISK REVERSAL EXAMPLE

The most obvious example of risk reversal in action is a money-back guarantee. This is quite common but might not be the best option in many cases. If you're undertaking a big project it would be hard for you to offer a full money-back guarantee, as that could bankrupt your company if things went wrong.

But there are other ways of reducing the risk in these situations. Here's how I used risk reversal many times. If I were in front of a prospect who was considering using us for a project, then I would offer them this guarantee.

"We will work with you for one week totally at our risk. At the end of the week, if you don't think the people we put in are right for you then I'll either replace the people involved and give you another week free or we'll finish working together with no cost to you. *However, if at the end of the week you're happy to keep working with us, then I will charge you for the week."*

Every time I used this risk reversal guarantee I was able to unlock a sale. It immediately removed the risk from the prospect and put it on us to get things right. Yes, we stood to lose a week's revenue if we got it wrong, but that was a small risk in return for winning a new client. It's a very powerful way to remove doubt and hesitation from a prospect and it helped us win several new customers.

In all the time I used it the guarantee was only called in once. The customer didn't rate one of the people I put on the project. After a discussion with them, they were happy for me to replace them. We went on to work with them for a long time after that.

Risk reversal was a no-brainer. I lost a week's cost of that person but gained a good customer and six figures of revenue.

TASK TO COMPLETE

Develop risk reversals for each of your propositions. Make sure they will be perceived by your prospects as removing risk from them and putting it on you.

BIDDING COMPETITIVELY

BIDDING FOR PROJECTS

The Core Story is designed to position you as an authority, and you will sometimes win business without competing for it. Despite that, there will be many situations where you will have to bid for the work and go head to head against competitors.

For many larger companies, it is mandatory that they run a bidding process before awarding projects. There are two standard processes you will encounter:

> Request For Information (RFI)

> Request For Proposal (RFP)

There are also two other processes that you might encounter:

> Request For Tender (RFT)

> Request For Quotation (RFQ)

REQUESTS FOR INFORMATION

The purpose of a request for information (RFI) is to collect written information about the capabilities of various suppliers. Normally it follows a format that can be used for comparative purposes. An RFI is primarily used to gather information to help the requestor decide what steps to take next. RFIs are therefore seldom the final stage and are instead often used in combination with RFPs, RFTs, and RFQs.

REQUESTS FOR PROPOSAL

A request for proposal (RFP) is a document that an organization posts to elicit bids from potential vendors for a desired IT solution. The RFP specifies what the requestor is looking for and establishes valuation criteria for assessing proposals.

An RFP generally includes background on the issuing organization and its lines of business, a set of specifications that describe the sought-after solution, and evaluation criteria that disclose how proposals will be graded. RFPs may also include a statement of work, which describes the tasks to be performed by the winning bidder and a timeline for providing deliverables.

WHAT TO DO WITH THEM?

It's very easy to get excited when you receive an RFI or RFP out of the blue. You can build up your hopes that you could win a big project.

The reality is that RFIs can go out to dozens of companies. The requestor will often put together a list of as many suppliers as they can and will then send the RFI to each supplier.

So, if you unexpectedly receive an RFI or RFP, don't assume that you've been specially selected. The opposite is most likely true: You're just one of many companies receiving it.

Similarly, RFPs often go out to 10 or more companies after the initial RFI numbers have been whittled down.

Here's my default advice when you receive RFIs & RFPs in the early days of your business. Run a mile in the other direction! They will waste humungous amounts of your time. And you will never win the work anyway.

Leave them to the larger companies, particularly when it's a big project. These companies will have dedicated people to respond to these requests. Particularly avoid RFPs where the winner will specifically be chosen based on the lowest price.

"RFPs are like a colonoscopy: Someone you don't even know gets to inspect you from the inside out. Sorry, I prefer to have dinner first."

Kevin Springer – Proposify

DIRTY SECRETS YOU SHOULD KNOW

There are some dirty little secrets to do with RFIs & RFPs that are important to know about.

Some companies use the process to gather information without ever intending to award a project. Some companies also use the process to get additional bids solely to put pressure on an existing supplier to reduce their prices. And the biggest and dirtiest secret is that some companies already know who is going to win the bid but they just have to show that they went through a formal bidding process.

Not all bidding processes take place on a level playing field

The buyers in these companies will feed secret information, hints, and suggestions to the company they want to win. Other bidders will never have a real chance of winning.

RFI/RFP BIDDING EXCEPTIONS

There are only very few occasions when you should respond to RFIs or RFPs.

1. If you helped put the RFP together! This happens more often than you would think
2. If you already have a relationship with the company
3. If you have a connection with the person running the bid
4. If you are on the inside track and have some inside information
5. If you are specifically asked to respond and you know that your bid is likely to be treated seriously
6. If the RFP is right in your sweet spot and you can find out that there are a very low number of bidders (three or fewer)
7. But still remain skeptical and be ready to pull out if you sense that you can't win.

SUMMARY OF THE RFI & RFP PROCESSES

Treat random RFIs RFPs with deep suspicion, skepticism and even derision. They can suck you dry and create false hope.

Respond to an RFI if you can do it with little effort and only respond to RFPs when you have one or more strong advantages.

RESPONDING TO RFPS

TIPS FOR RFP RESPONSES

Assuming that you've got a strong reason to respond to an RFP, you'll need to follow some procedures to increase your chances of winning the work.

Whether you're responding to an RFP or responding directly to a prospect's request, you will have to put a proposal together.

The following tips are good guidelines to follow. These tips are mostly aimed at RFP responses but can equally apply to non-competitive proposals.

ALWAYS RESPOND ON TIME. DUH!

Every RFP will have a deadline date for the response.

Don't miss it.

This is basic 101 stuff, but most big bids receive proposals after the deadline.

If this happens to you, I will guarantee one outcome. You *will* get disqualified no matter how good your proposal is. And you will have wasted weeks of effort.

MEET *ALL* MANDATORY REQUIREMENTS

This is more basic 101 stuff.

Every RFP will have a set of mandatory requirements that need to be met. If you can't meet them, you shouldn't be responding.

You *will* get disqualified no matter how good your proposal is. And you will have wasted weeks of effort.

SPELLCHECK, SPELLCHECK, SPELLCHECK

Typos and shoddy formatting will kill your chances and you will have wasted weeks of effort.

Have multiple people review the document. Implement a four-eyes policy as a minimum to ensure that your response is the best it can be.

RESPOND IN THE CORRECT FORMAT

If the RFP requires you to submit a printed document by hand or by post, then make sure you do that. Don't make the mistake of only submitting an electronic version. You *will* get disqualified. No matter how good your proposal is. And you will have wasted weeks of effort.

USE A TEMPLATE TO PROVIDE CONSISTENCY

Your proposal is a window into your organization. Make sure it represents your brand well. If you haven't got a branded template, then source one or get one designed on an outsourcing site. It's okay to have standard sections pre-prepared, but make sure each RFP gets a personalized response.

COMMIT THE RESOURCES

If you decide to respond, then take it seriously and make sure you do a good job. Set aside the time and eliminate distractions. Support those tasked with responding. It's always a team effort.

MIRROR THE RFP'S STRUCTURE

The RFP will be laid out with chapters and sections in a logical flow as defined by the requestor. They will have spent weeks/months preparing it so they will be very familiar with its structure. It gives you a ready-made structure for your response. Make sure that you follow the sections and numbering and refer to these in your response. Doing this will make it easier for readers to follow and understand your response.

RESPOND BASED ON THE EVALUATION CRITERIA

RFPs often have criteria by which responses will be evaluated. Make sure you respond according to these criteria. Don't try to steer your response to the criteria that you would like to be evaluated on.

WOW THEM WITH ADDITIONAL VALUE

Go beyond just meeting the RFP issuer's needs. Add in any extra information to enhance the proposal and show them that you are willing to go beyond the call of duty. Can you spot any gaps in the RFP that you could fill? This could be a unique advantage if others don't spot it.

NB: This assumes that there's no stated restriction to doing this.

OFFER OPTIONS

If you think there are different ways to achieve the desired outcome, then offer some options to enhance your proposal.

Option 1 must be the required/mandatory requirements. Make sure that you meet these first before offering other options.

Additional options can add value, be cheaper, better, or even more expensive solutions.

Offering options could be your chance to show your real expertise and competitive advantage.

NB: This assumes that there's no stated restriction to doing this.

LEAVE ROOM TO NEGOTIATE

Any price you quote will not be the final price accepted no matter how much you think it is or want it to be. Leave some room for negotiation.

The purchasing department will be expected to get a deal from you, so you will need some wiggle room to let them "win." But you should only concede under "duress." Never make it look like you've over-inflated your price.

DON'T BANKRUPT YOUR BUSINESS

If the prospective customer responds asking for a lower price that will hurt your business, you'll want to politely bow out of the running. Sometimes you have to walk away from a bid if the price they're prepared to pay is too low. Some tough negotiators like to try to push suppliers to the brink because then they know they've got the lowest price possible. Make sure your brink still has some profit in it.

PRESENTING YOUR PROPOSAL

YOUR CHANCE TO SHINE

With an RFP, the normal process is that you submit your proposal and then, after a period of review by the prospect, you'll hear if you've made the shortlist.

Those shortlisted normally get a chance to present their proposal to the prospect's decision-makers. This is your chance to shine and to show the prospect why you should be selected as the winner.

PRESENTING GUIDELINES

The following tips are great guidelines to follow if you get shortlisted and have the opportunity to present your proposal. They are mostly aimed at RFP presentations but can equally apply to any presentations you have to do to a prospect.

PRESENT AS A TEAM

For big projects, I recommend that you present as a team. Prospects like to meet with some of the key people who might be used on the project, so bring your best customer-friendly people with you. They can answer some questions and help you out if you get stuck. The more you can show your expertise across different aspects of the project the more chance you have of winning the deal.

TURN UP ON TIME. DUH!

You've worked your butt off to put together a great proposal and to get shortlisted. Don't blow it by turning up late for the presentation.

When you get invited to present your proposal you should expect to be presenting to a group of people who are all stakeholders in the project. This group can include users, IT infrastructure people, directors, support staff, etc. If you turn up late, you're going to have a whole group of people unhappy with you for delaying the presentation. You will be on the back foot right from the get-go. In some cases, you might lose your chance to present which will ultimately cost you the opportunity to work with the prospect.

Your competitors will turn up on time. Why would you
give them an advantage by being late?

Even if you are still allowed to present you will have created the wrong impression from the start. You will also be time-constrained and may not be able to deliver your full presentation or handle questions. Travel early so that there's very little chance of being late. Stay overnight nearby if you have to.

I would often arrange to meet with our presenting team in a local coffee shop an hour before the presentation. This gave us a chance to review our plans for the presentation and allowed us to arrive relaxed and ready to go at the appointed time.

GET STRAIGHT TO THE POINT

The audience will most likely be seeing multiple presentations on the same day. They want to hear what you bring to the party. Quickly!

Don't fill your presentation with fluff. Hit all the main points of your presentation particularly the mandatory requirements. Tell them how you plan to deliver the project on time and to budget.

Emphasize your expertise and why you're the best company to carry out the project. In particular, talk about some of the unique things that you can bring to the project that others can't.

SELL THE VISION

The prospect will have a vision for how the project will help their business. Make sure you replay that vision back to them and tell them how you will help them achieve their goals.

Will you help them beat their competitors?

Will you help them win new customers?

Will you help them enter new markets?

Will you help them increase their customer retention?

Will you help them increase profit margins?

Will you help them reduce costs?

ADDRESS THEIR UNSPOKEN QUESTIONS

The people you are presenting to will have numerous unspoken questions in their minds. Answers to these questions will help them make decisions about which company they will choose to work with.

When they are listening to you present your proposal, they will be assessing you with these thoughts in mind:

- Do you understand their business challenges?
- Do you have the capability to deliver the project?
- Do you have their best interests at heart?
- How will you get them from where they are now to where they want to be?
- What results will they see?
- How will you work with them?
- Why would you be the best choice for them?

Make sure that your presentation addresses these unspoken questions and leaves them with a positive feeling about you.

THERE COULD BE NEGATIVITY IN THE ROOM

Occasionally when you present to a group of people you will encounter some negativity from one or more of the people on the evaluation team. In a room full of people not everybody is guaranteed to be neutral or even positive toward you and your company.

If other companies have presented their proposals before you, then some of the evaluation team may have already decided that they prefer one of these other proposers.

They may ask difficult questions to try and knock you off your stride. How you handle these questions is important to how your presentation will be received.

Build rapport if you can by acknowledging the question. Give friendly answers and smile. Don't let these negative people deflect you from doing a great job.

If you get a difficult question that you or your team don't know the answer to then just be honest and say that you don't know but that you can find out for them.

The worst thing you can do in these situations is to waffle and give a weak, or even wrong, answer. You'll get far more respect for being honest and saying you don't know.

THERE COULD BE BAD BODY LANGUAGE

Occasionally you will do a presentation where one or more people will look bored or inattentive. They might have sat through several presentations that day so their attention span will have waned.

Some people might be on their cell phones or laptops and some may even answer a call. Somebody could fall asleep during your presentation. This happened one time when we made a presentation to a large Japanese company. One of the directors had been out for lunch and had drunk some wine and struggled to stay awake during our presentation.

There's little that you can do to control other people's behavior, so don't let it deflect you from delivering a great presentation.

ENCOURAGE QUESTIONS AND DISCUSSION

Pick points in your presentation where you stop and ask a pertinent question. Good questions can be used to demonstrate your expertise and/or to confirm that you are on track with your understanding of their needs.

TELL STORIES

Human beings are programmed to respond to stories. Stories help us to pay attention, and also to remember things. If you can use stories in your presentation, your audience is more likely to engage and to remember your points afterward.

If you're a new business, then tell stories from your previous jobs. You are the sum of all your previous experience, so a good story from your past can still be relevant and a great way to get a point across.

REHEARSE REHEARSE REHEARSE

One golden rule we implemented was that we would always rehearse for important presentations. The bigger the project the more rehearsing you should do.

Do dummy run-throughs of your presentation so that you know what's on each slide, what comes next, timings, etc. Have other people play the roles that you're likely to face. Give them permission to ask difficult questions and to interrupt you.

> *Practice answering difficult questions so that you have*
> *good answers for them*

If you know that you're not strong in one or more areas of the project, then you can anticipate some questions that you might be asked. Make sure that you can give a good credible answer in these situations.

HOW TO STAND OUT

Some years ago, we were bidding to win a multi-million-dollar project. We were one of three companies chosen to present our proposal. The other companies we were competing against were much bigger than us, so we knew it would be difficult to beat them and win the project.

I needed a way to make us stand out against these much bigger competitors, so I came up with an idea that made us look different and demonstrated how keen we were to win the project.

It worked and we won the project. That customer subsequently spent north of $15 million with us. We also won another multi-million-dollar project in the same sector because of the experience we gained with that customer.

DO SOMETHING UNUSUAL TO WOW THEM

If you can do something that makes you different and memorable, then you can greatly enhance your chances of winning the project.

When we were pitching for the multi-million-dollar project we identified a part of the system that we could mock up. It was a manual barcoding process in a warehouse.

We put together a prototype of the application we intended building and we borrowed a barcoding device. We also got a few sample grading sacks with barcodes on them and a scales to weigh the contents. We brought a separate laptop with us to do the mockup on. We had it set up so that it looked like the barcoding device was connected to the prototype we'd built.

At an appropriate point in the presentation, we stopped and ran through the mockup in front of the prospect's evaluation team. We did a role-play showing how a warehouse person would scan and weigh the bags and how that would register in the system.

This got everybody's attention and it allowed us to demonstrate our understanding of their requirements. I knew from the vibe in the room, and from the questions that we got asked, that we had hit a home run.

I subsequently found out that the mockup and role-play was a key factor in helping us win the project. We gained kudos for spending some of our own money and time to create the mockup.

This was the big differentiator between us and the other two bidders, and it enabled us to land a new customer that would go on to spend millions of dollars with us.

So, my advice is this. Ask yourself if there is anything that you can do that would make you different when presenting your proposal.

If it's a big project, then it could be worth it to invest some time and money to enhance your bid.

Some things you could consider include:

- Do a role-play
- Show a prototype you've built for free
- Mock-up one of the outputs of the solution

Find something to get them to pay attention and to make you stand out. If it's something that gets a laugh, then that's okay as long as it's not cringeworthy!

Going the extra mile at this stage shows that you really want to win. That's a positive thing to leave them with. And know this. Very few (if any) of your competitors will use this idea.

NB: This all assumes that there is nothing stated in the RFP that would prevent you from using this idea.

FINANCIAL CONTROL

BEYOND THE LAUNCH PHASE

Up to this point, the focus of this book has been on how you can launch your business and win your first customer(s). That's stage one of building a successful business. But to get to seven figures, and beyond, you have to run the business in a financially sound way if you're going to stay around for the long term.

MY ESSENTIAL RULES OF FINANCE

Over the many years that I ran my business, I learned a lot of lessons about managing the financial aspects of the business.

I started with very little experience in financial management and I made plenty of mistakes along the way, but as each year went by my experience grew. Along the way, I developed a set of rules that guided me as we successfully grew the business to multiple millions of revenues annually.

REVENUE ≠ PROFIT ≠ CASH

You must understand the difference between revenue, profit, and cash if you are going to build a successful business.

You can have good revenues but you can still be making a loss if your costs are greater than your income.

You can be very profitable but you can still run out of cash if you don't get paid on time.

You can have good cash balances but you can be burning the cash if you're not generating profits or getting paid on time.

AVOID DEBT LIKE THE PLAGUE

Some people will disagree with this one, but I recommend that you don't take on any debt, particularly in the early days of the business.

Having debt can be like a millstone around your neck. If you must take on debt, then do so sparingly and repay it quickly.

AIM FOR GROSS MARGINS OF **50%** OR MORE

We'll talk about numbers in a later chapter, but for now just know that you must target 50% in gross margins if you're going to run a profitable and growing business.

PRICE PROJECTS IN PHASES TO MINIMIZE RISK

One of your most important roles when running a business is to manage risk. When taking on a fixed-price project you will have to carefully assess the risk so that you don't underprice the project and end up making a loss, which could ultimately damage your business.

Risk management is vital when pricing projects.

My preferred way to do this is to price projects in phases whenever possible. This limits the total exposure you're likely to have. It can also limit the exposure the customer has too.

I nearly always start by pricing a discovery phase, as this can be time-limited. It's also your chance to discover everything you need to know about the project and enables you to price subsequent phases more accurately. Note that it won't always be possible to do this especially if you are responding to RFPs. In these cases, you will have to load your estimates or quotes with contingency. I'll discuss this further in a later chapter.

AVOID DISCOUNTING IF AT ALL POSSIBLE

Offering discounts is the first resort of the weak-willed. It shows that they lack confidence in what they are selling. If you're seen to easily drop your prices it could compromise your integrity and you might never be trusted by the prospect again. It also sets a precedent in the prospect's mind that your pricing isn't firm and that everything can be discounted. You are selling a high-quality B2B professional service.

Customers are paying for your expertise, so you need to charge appropriately.

Having said all that, there are occasions when offering a discount can make sense. But here's my rule for when you should discount

Only trade a discount for something valuable in return.

The keyword here is "trade." You're offering a discount in return for something—shorter payment terms, for example. In my experience, the more aggressive a prospect is at trying to secure a discount from you the more likely they are to become a difficult customer. They're also more likely to be late payers too.

SET PAYMENT TERMS TO 30 DAYS OR FEWER

This is probably the single most important financial rule to obey. Negotiating your payment terms is one thing you must become good at if you're not going to burn cash.

INVOICE IMMEDIATELY

The payment terms you agree to will often only take effect from the point where the customer receives your invoice. So, make sure to invoice them on the agreed day and get the invoice to them as soon as possible.

GET PAID ON TIME. RELIGIOUSLY!

It's one thing to have agreed on payment terms. It's a completely different thing to get paid in accordance with those terms.

It's your job to make sure that you get paid on the agreed date. Don't assume the customer will always pay on time.

Not every customer will pay you on time, no matter what the contract says. If this happens then chase payment hard and keep at it until you get paid.

If the payment hasn't hit your account on time, then you should politely but firmly inquire why not and then keep pursuing it until you have been paid.

NEGOTIATE STAGED PAYMENTS

If you can't negotiate regular payments based on elapsed time periods, then aim to negotiate stage payments based on agreed deliverables.

The smaller these deliverables are the more frequently you can deliver them—and the better your cash flow will be.

CHARGE AN UPFRONT FEE IF YOU CAN

Many contracts have initial payments, or setup fees, included. This is a good way to improve your cash flow. If you do have to offer a discount you could do so in return for some form of upfront payment.

AIM FOR SIX MONTHS OF WORKING CAPITAL

As your business grows and you start making profits you should be conservative about taking money out of the company. Resist the urge to start paying yourself a bigger and bigger salary or taking big dividends.

Your first goal should be to build up your cash reserves and a good target is to aim to have six months working capital in reserve. This will enable you to comfortably run the business without having to panic if, for instance, a customer doesn't pay you on time.

Build up a war chest of cash to protect your business
from unexpected events.

Over a period of years, I built up our cash reserves to well over $1 million. It enabled us to weather all sorts of unexpected events and various economic cycles. Having good cash reserves meant that I never had to lie awake at night worrying about cash and whether I could afford to pay our staff.

The Covid-19 outbreak is an example of a situation that you can't foresee but which can have a critical effect on your business. Many companies will have gone bust because they didn't have enough cash to weather the storm. Well-run companies will always have reserves of cash to see them through challenging situations. Make sure that you're one of these companies.

ALWAYS FILE AND PAY YOUR TAXES ON TIME

As I mentioned in the introduction, I didn't file my first tax return on time. I knew we had no tax to pay so I didn't think I needed to file a return. We ended up getting an inspection visit from the tax authorities and we were flagged for observation. That was a mistake I never made again.

Here's my strong advice. You don't want to unnecessarily appear on your tax authority's radar. There are few things more stressful in business than a visit from the tax authority. File and pay your taxes on time and be a compliant company. Your life will be much smoother that way.

THE BUCK STOPS WITH YOU

If you're going to run a company, you will have to learn the basics of accounting. As the leader of the company, the buck will stop with you, so you will need to understand the financial aspects of the business.

The basics of accounting are easy to learn. A software development business is a relatively simple business to manage. There are usually no big assets to worry about. It's primarily about monitoring the profit and loss and the cash flow.

One thing that catches a lot of young companies out is the management of taxes. Whether it's local, state or national taxes you need to both record these correctly and report them correctly. As I mentioned previously, make sure that you pay them on time, or else you could be visited by the authorities.

As your business grows your accounting may become more complex. You may acquire equipment or other assets, you may register intellectual property, you may take on debt, etc. Most of these items find their way on to the balance sheet, so learning how to read both a profit and loss statement and a balance sheet are two skills you should aim to acquire.

KNOW YOUR NUMBERS

If you're going to run a profitable business, then you will have to understand some key numbers. Here are the most important numbers you should understand.

STAFF COSTS

The biggest expense in any service business is the cost of staff.

Remember, staff will also cost you benefits, employer taxes, and they will require equipment to operate, so knowing the fully loaded cost for each employee is really important when it comes to setting your rates.

COST OF GOODS SOLD (COGS)

In a pure services business, the main item that falls under COGS is staff costs. You may also have contractor/consultant costs if you use non-employee resources.

OVERHEADS AND EXPENSES

Overheads and expenses are all the costs that are associated with running the business and will include rent, utilities, phones, marketing, supplies, travel, etc.

GROSS PROFIT (GP)

Gross profit is a money amount that is your revenue less the cost of goods sold. So, whatever you earn on a job you deduct the COGS to leave your gross profit. Many laypeople think gross profit is the bottom line profit a company makes. That is wrong. It's net profit that's the most important number. To make a net profit you must have a gross profit that is greater than your overheads and expenses.

GROSS MARGIN (GM%)

Gross margin is the difference between revenue and cost of goods sold divided by revenue, expressed as a percentage. So, if you earn $600 and your COGS are $300 then your gross margin is 50%.

NET PROFIT

Net profit is your bottom-line figure. It is calculated as

(revenue – cost of goods sold – overheads – taxes – interest).

When all is said and done this is the number that tells you whether you're making money or not.

DEBTOR DAYS

Debtor days is the average number of days required for you to receive payment from your customers for invoices issued to them. It is vital to manage your debtor days closely especially in your early days when cash is tight.

The longer you wait to get paid the more cash you will need available to operate the business until you get paid. Many companies get into trouble because their debtor days number is too big. They don't collect cash quickly enough and then run out of money. This is why paying attention to your payment terms is so important. I'll discuss this in a later chapter.

CASH FLOW

Cash flow is the difference between the available cash at the beginning of an accounting period and that at the end of the period.

Cash flow can be increased by selling more goods or services, selling an asset, reducing costs, increasing the selling price, collecting debts faster, paying creditors slower, bringing in more equity or taking a loan.

Cash flow can be decreased by paying for operating and direct expenses, debt servicing, and the purchase of an asset.

The level of cash flow is not necessarily a good measure of performance, and vice versa: High levels of cash flow do not necessarily mean high or even any profit.

Equally, high levels of profit do not automatically translate into high or even positive cash flow.

TASK TO COMPLETE

If you lack experience in the bookkeeping field then go and get yourself a copy of a book such as *Bookkeeping & Accounting All-In-One For Dummies* or spend a few hours on YouTube educating yourself.

This will be time well spent and you'll be forever thankful that you invested this time once your business starts growing.

PRICING YOUR SERVICES

PRICING FOR PROFIT

A core part of your business plan will be deciding how to price your services. Factors that will come into play are your competitors' rates, the uniqueness of your offering, the market demand for your services, the capacity of your customers to pay, etc.

To grow a business, you need to charge prices that cover overheads and expenses as well as paying salaries. You also need to make a profit if you're going to be able to pay yourself dividends, invest in future growth, and if you want to eventually sell your business.

Your expenses might be low when you're bootstrapping, but you need to position your prices for when you have more staff, office space, and other overheads.

It's very hard to significantly uplift your prices in the future, especially with existing customers, so aim to set your rates high enough at the beginning.

Competing on price is a race to the bottom. That's a race you never want to win.

When I started my business, I knew that I didn't want to compete at the lower end of the market by charging low rates. There are lots of software companies prepared to cut their rates to win business, but that game is a race to the bottom. Eventually, they go out of business. I also knew that I would find it hard to justify the very high-end rates that some of the big consultancies charge.

I knew from experience, and through my connections, what the average daily rate that most software companies were charging, so I went with a rate schedule that was above this average by about 20%, i.e., more expensive than most other software companies. The rate schedule had rates from low to high for different skill levels such as junior developer, senior developer, analyst, delivery manager, etc. When pricing a job, I would then combine different skill levels at different rates.

Remember, the more effort you put into your core story and the better niche positioning you have then the easier it will be to charge a premium price.

AVOID THE BIG PRICING MISTAKE

If you've worked in the software industry for any length of time, then you will probably have a good idea of how much freelance contractors' day rates are for your skillset.

There can be a temptation to use those rates as the basis for your prices. That would be a *big mistake*.

> *Do not try to compete on price with freelancers. You will struggle to build a seven-figure business if you do.*

You must *avoid at all costs competing with freelancers*. Remember, you're not in the freelancing business! You are building a professional services business with a range of skills and capabilities and you are aiming to take on a portfolio of customers.

You will be able to offer customers more value than a freelancer can. You will be able to take on bigger projects and to offer a broader range of skills. You can both project manage and deliver new solutions using your teams. You will also be able to offer ongoing support and maintenance contracts for the work you do.

NEGOTIATION

BECOMING A GOOD NEGOTIATOR

One skill that you will want to develop is negotiation. Learning how to negotiate is a fundamental skill required to build a successful business.

You may not be aware of it, but you're constantly negotiating outcomes in your daily life, whether you're trying to get a raise from your boss or trying to get your spouse or partner to do something or trying to get your kids to behave. All of these involve the art of negotiation.

By developing your negotiation skills, you will give yourself a greater chance of maintaining your profit margins and managing risk while building great customer relationships.

You will also need good negotiation skills to be able to deal with your staff and your suppliers.

WHAT IS NEGOTIATION?

Negotiation is about knowing what you want and going after it while still respecting the other person or party in the process.

Remember that the whole point of negotiating is compromise.

This means that you need to look out for yourself, but you should also be willing to budge in order to satisfy both parties.

The real skill in negotiating is to build professional
relationships rather than burning bridges on your way
out of the meeting room.

Negotiation is *not* about one side winning and the other side losing. That is not how you build long-term relationships. Negotiation should be all about creating a win-win situation. The worst outcome in a negotiation is win-lose or lose-win. It's okay to negotiate hard, but you must always be fair and respectful. If you find yourself being pushed into a win-lose situation then it may be time to walk away.

YOUR VITAL NEEDS

In any negotiation, there will be vital needs on both sides of the fence. There will be certain things that fall into the must-have category. These vital needs will rarely be conceded or altered without a tough fight.

When it comes to your vital needs there are a number of key points that you should always try to achieve.

- Payment terms: maximum of 30 days
- Stage payments: either monthly or at regular intervals
- Upfront payment: if you can get this then great
- Retention: maximum of 10% and always time-limited

PAYMENT TERMS

Negotiating favorable payment terms is one of your most important goals on all contracts. You must protect your cash flow and ensure that you get paid within 30 days or fewer. Resist hard against any attempt to get you to accept longer payment terms. It's far better to yield on other things to keep 30-day payment terms.

Remember that the payment terms take effect from the invoice date. Typically, you'll work for some weeks then you'll submit your invoice. So, from the time you begin the work to the time you receive payment could be at least 60 days even with 30-day payment terms.

So, always be aware that bad payment terms could turn a potentially profitable deal into a disaster because of cash flow problems.

STAGE PAYMENTS

Make sure to have regular payments built into the contract. You need to keep cash flowing as a project progresses. I always pushed for monthly billing and I nearly always got it.

Otherwise, tie payment to short deliverables. You could tie payments to sprints for example. This would enable you to get paid regularly.

Just make sure that you don't have elongated periods without payment or it will kill your cash flow.

Unless ....

UPFRONT PAYMENT

On some contracts, it is possible to negotiate an upfront payment. It is usually payable on signing the contract.

Typically, it will be about 10% of the contract value. It could also be a specific sum. Take any chance you can to negotiate an upfront payment. If you're being forced to accept some other less-advantageous clause, then trade a concession for an upfront payment.

RETENTION

On many projects, particularly larger projects, customers will want to retain some payment for a period to undergo acceptance testing. Whenever you can you will want to try and avoid having a retention clause in the contract so never volunteer or offer a retention period. Let the customer ask for it. Never allow this to be more than 10% of the contract value. Negotiate for 5% as best as you can.

The danger with a retention period is that it could run on forever, so you need to negotiate hard to get this time-limited. I always tried to get it limited to 30 days. I didn't always succeed but I nearly always got a limit on it.

I also learned a valuable lesson after one customer put a system into production but still held on to the retention money saying that they were still testing the system. From that point forward I always had a clause in our contracts which stated that if they went live with the system, then it was deemed to be accepted and the retention period was finished.

NEGOTIATION TIPS

Having been involved in well over 100 contract negotiations I've learned quite a few things and I've developed my negotiation skills so that I can comfortably operate at any level in business. Here are some of my best tips for you.

KEEP EGOS OUT OF IT

Never turn negotiation into a battle of egos. Avoid using I or me all the time. Use collaborative language like we/us/our a lot. So, for instance, say "how we can reach a solution" instead of "I want ..."

BUILD RAPPORT

Never go into negotiations in a confrontational mood. It's unlikely to end well. Your goal is to build rapport with the other party right from the beginning of negotiations.

Human connection is paramount in negotiation, and your attitude and energy going in will set the tone and affect the outcome.

If you go in anticipating a war, that's exactly what you'll experience.

On the flip side, if you go into the negotiation with the intention of making a deal that satisfies the interests of both parties, you're much more likely to have that outcome.

FOCUS ON WIN-WIN

If you approach a negotiation thinking only of yourself, then you will lose deals you should have won, or you'll end up with a bad outcome for the other party. Understanding what all parties need, and working for all concerned, is a vital strategy in negotiations.

Ultimately, all people involved should find themselves on the same side of the fence. There should be a shared commitment to delivering the project and achieving the anticipated outcomes.

Keep your eye on the big picture and don't get caught up in the small stuff. There are lots of things that need to be negotiated in a contract, much of it small stuff that should be quickly and easily agreed upon.

Avoid making a big issue of these small things. If you find yourself getting dragged into tough conversations on some of the minor things, then you can diffuse the situation by making some simple concessions or by trading one small item against another.

ALWAYS BE WILLING TO NEGOTIATE

Be very careful about being intransigent and backing yourself into a corner by being unwilling to negotiate a certain point.

> *Stubbornness or intransigence will rarely get you anywhere in negotiations.*

Many negotiations in business, politics and general life get broken off because of one side's stubbornness or intransigence. Yes, there will be things that you want to hold firm on, but that doesn't mean that you can't negotiate your way around them. A great way to negotiate a tough point is to show flexibility by presenting some alternative options.

If you show that you're looking to find an outcome that works for both sides, then you're more likely to get the other party to explore the alternative options.

NO DOESN'T ALWAYS MEAN NO

In negotiations, there is a lot of posturing and partial truth. Typically, both sides will reserve their position in the early negotiations until they see how things progress. So, when the other party says No, sometimes it's a way of preserving their position until further negotiations have taken place. If both parties are committed to a deal then most things are negotiable. You just need to find the key to unlock a Yes.

DON'T UNDERESTIMATE YOUR STRENGTH

In a negotiation, no side holds all the aces. It's easy to focus on your perceived weaknesses and to let that dominate your actions during the negotiations. But if you do that, you'll likely agree to a deal that is not the best one that you could have got.

The very fact the customer is negotiating with you shows that you have something they want, so you're likely to have a more powerful position in the negotiations than you think.

Do you know what pressures/deadlines are on the other side? They might need your services more than you realize.

Do you know what alternatives the customer might have? They might not be a great option for them.

Do you know the advantages you have over your competitors in the deal? These advantages might give you a strong hand.

DON'T OVERESTIMATE YOUR POSITION

Never act as if you hold a dominant position in negotiations. Prospects will detect this and will react accordingly.

Nobody likes being forced into a position of weakness in negotiations. If you do that, then you run a big risk of losing the deal entirely.

No matter how strong you think your hand is there will still be things that you don't know about the other party's position. They may have an alternative to your offer that you don't know about.

AIM HIGHER THAN YOU'D BE SATISFIED WITH

Don't be afraid to ask for certain things and to aim higher than you want. For example, you could ask for 14-day payment terms and let them negotiate it to 30 days. That way you can seem to concede to them, but you might get something else in return for that concession.

NEVER NEGOTIATE OUT OF DESPERATION

No matter how badly you need the work, never show desperation by conceding lots of things. You'll live to regret it and you may end up with a loss-making deal on your hands.

Hold your air of authority and negotiate from a position of strength. Focus on what you bring to the table and how the prospect will be better off working with you.

IT'S OK TO PUSH BACK

You show strength by occasionally pushing back on certain things to show to the other side what is important to you. This helps set some boundaries for the discussions. But you can then yield on some of these pushbacks later to agree on a more important item.

YIELD RELUCTANTLY

Sometimes you need to yield on a point, but it can help do that reluctantly. You can make it seem that the concession was a big thing for you. Yielding reluctantly is a way of letting the other side feel like they won a small victory in the negotiations. But you can use that compromise later in your favor.

ALWAYS NEGOTIATE WITH A DECISION-MAKER

This is a mistake I made more than once in the early days of my business.

I assumed that I was negotiating with somebody who had the power to sign off on the deal, but I later discovered he had to present it to his manager for approval. In situations like this, it is easy to negotiate the deal and to make what you believe are final concessions only to find that the higher authority wants further concessions, discounts, etc.

One of the early principles you want to establish when negotiating is that you are dealing with the final decision maker(s).

If you're not, then you will have to be careful about your starting point and how much you're willing to concede before the final negotiations.

It's quite common in large corporations for a senior person to negotiate a deal and then pass it over to the purchasing department, which is tasked with getting further discounts and concessions, before proceeding with final ratification.

DEVELOP YOUR NEGOTIATION SKILLS

Negotiation is one of those skills that you will get better at as you do more of it.

You should also invest some time in developing your negotiation skills. It will pay you back handsomely as you get better at striking deals.

Here are a couple of books I recommend you read.

Influence: the Psychology of Persuasion by Robert Cialdini

Negotiation Genius: How to Overcome Obstacles and Achieve Brilliant Results at the Bargaining Table and Beyond by Deepak Malhotra and Max Bazerman

OPERATING THE BUSINESS

GETTING THE RIGHT INFRASTRUCTURE

Getting the business launched is one thing, but once you start acquiring customers you need to ensure that your business operates efficiently and profitably if you're going to get to seven figures and more. You will need to have a good infrastructure to help support your business activities. There are a number of systems you should look at putting in place as early as possible.

TIME AND EXPENSE RECORDING

Right from the get-go, I knew that we would need some systems in place to ensure that we could operate our business efficiently.

I knew from my previous experience that a timesheet system is essential for any services business, so I made sure that we put one in place. This was in 1996 when the Internet was starting to explode. At that time, I wanted to ensure that we had a web-based solution so that developers working at customer sites could complete their timesheets.

At that stage there were no commercially available web-based timesheet applications, so I set about writing one. Twenty years later that same application, with some modifications, was still being used by our company.

Without a timesheet system you cannot know how much to bill a customer, nor do you have any metrics for measuring productivity or analyzing time spent against estimates.

It is a core piece of infrastructure that you should have in place from day zero.

It's very difficult to introduce time recording after the
business has been running for a while.
Do it from the beginning.

One consistent problem I've seen over the years is that service companies that don't implement timesheet recording right from the beginning of the business eventually find it very difficult to introduce it at a later stage because of resistance from staff. It's very hard to get people to change their ways if they are not used to recording time.

I dealt with that issue by having time recording in place right from the beginning. I also made a big point of emphasizing the importance of timesheets during staff inductions and I made sure that people were held accountable if they didn't complete them on time.

I also added an expense recording module to the timesheet system so that we could track expenses on customer projects.

We also used it to reimburse our staff for any out-of-pocket expenses they incurred during a project.

FINANCIAL MANAGEMENT

The next most important application we started with was our accounting system.

Before we had signed any business, I purchased a copy of QuickBooks and set it up for our type of services business.

It was vital to me that I knew, on a month-by-month basis, what our profit and loss figures were and to track and manage overheads and expenses.

Being able to track your finances on a month-by-month
basis is essential for the health of your business

As the company grew it became even more important to keep my finger on the pulse and to watch our costs and, most importantly, our cash collection and debtor days. It was also vital that we tracked our liabilities such as taxes and ensured that we provisioned for these.

It is often said that more companies go bust when they are growing rapidly than when they are struggling for growth. This is because their expenses start to outstrip their cash collection and they eventually run out of cash. They have plenty of revenue booked, but the cash is not coming in quickly enough to cover the expenses. Don't let that happen to you.

CRM

Another essential infrastructure component is a Customer Relationship Management (CRM) system.

We initially started with ACT but then transitioned to one of the first web-based CRM platforms, eWare, before eventually settling on Microsoft Dynamics after it was released. A CRM system was essential for us, as we were doing a lot of mailings and keeping track of all the outbound marketing, and inbound traffic would have been impossible without an integrated solution.

Today it is much easier to build the infrastructure you need using cloud services. You can quickly have a timesheet and expense system up and running without any need for software on-site.

There are also dozens of online accounting and CRM systems so there's no excuse for not having a good infrastructure.

OTHER OPERATIONAL SYSTEMS

There are also many more solutions available that will make your business life easier.

There are team communication and collaboration tools such as Skype, Zoom, Microsoft Teams, Slack, Trello, Asana, etc. Some of these are even free to use.

The key is to ensure that you get the important pieces in place *right from the start* and that you have processes for managing the business. Make sure that you can track time, expenses, overheads, billing, debtors, and, most important, cash collection at the press of a button.

TASKS TO COMPLETE

Make decisions about what systems you are going to use and then get them in place.

STAFFING

YOUR BIGGEST INVESTMENT

The biggest investment you'll make in your business will be in your staff. So you need to get it right.

To be competitive and to have a good balance you need a range of staff at different cost levels.

As a small company, you can't afford to have difficult or negative people on board. You need to hire people who are willing to be flexible.

You need to inculcate a can-do attitude in everybody. Nobody should ever say "That's not my job."

It all starts with the recruitment process.

RECRUITMENT

One of your most important tasks, especially in the early days, is to invest time in the recruitment process to make sure that you get the best people. If you treat recruitment as a pain in the ass or you try to take shortcuts, you will end up hiring the wrong people.

Never underestimate the importance of recruitment. It's one of your most important jobs, especially in the early days.

In the beginning, it's important that you, as the business owner, interview the candidates. You will be the company's best salesperson for new recruits, and you can make sure that the candidates are buying into your vision for the company.

Recruit for attitude and cultural fit first and foremost. These types of people will be easier to work with and will act as better representatives of your business.

You also need to hire people with good skills who can deliver great work to your customers and who you can delegate responsibility to.

Your goal is to build a team of trusted lieutenants who will do a great job for you while you continue building the company. You want motivated people who you don't have to micro-manage.

The key to getting it right is to implement a recruitment process. As a first step, you should put together a set of test questions to filter out weak candidates. You'll need different questions for different roles.

When we first did this, we were amazed at how many developers didn't know some basic things. Our test helped us filter out people who wouldn't have been good recruits for us because of their weak development skills.

Make sure that you get references for each candidate and follow them up if you intend to make an offer. This is especially true for senior people, as you could end up making a very costly mistake if they turn out to be a bad hire.

INDUCTION

A process that is overlooked by many companies is induction. There's nothing worse than joining a new company only to find yourself lost on the first day. It's vital to have a formal induction process for new staff. *Don't* dump them in at the deep end on day one.

Plan for their arrival. You will know a few weeks in advance when they are starting so there's no excuse not to be prepared. Have a desk and computer configured and ready. Have their login and email accounts already set up for them.

Book meetings in their diary so when they open their calendar they'll see that they have induction meetings with various people.

Plan to spend some quality time with each new recruit on the morning they arrive. Build a presentation that you walk new hires through. Talk about your core values. Explain what's expected of them and what they can expect of you. This is your chance to get them excited about the opportunity ahead.

STAFF AUGMENTATION

It doesn't always make sense to hire full-time recruits. To stay profitable you will often need to use some non-employee resources on projects.

You need to build in flexibility to account for bench time. There will be times when your workload drops off, particularly at the end of projects, so you need to be able to cut expenses accordingly.

This is where it helps to have contract staff as part of your resource pool. I always aimed for about a 20% "squidge" factor i.e. at least 20% of my staff were on short-term contracts. This meant that I could reduce my costs quickly if the workload changed.

FIRING STAFF

As a small company, you can't carry poor performers or negative/difficult people. They will bleed your time and will cause issues with customers and projects. In the worst cases, they will cost you money and damage your reputation.

As the head of the company, your role is to protect your business and your reputation. Sometimes that means that you have to make some tough decisions.

In such scenarios, it's essential to act decisively. Any time I delayed making a decision I subsequently regretted it and I still went through with the dismissal months later when even more damage had occurred.

Don't carry poorly performing staff out of sentimentality or a sense of loyalty. They will only stress you out and cause you problems. They can also cause issues with other staff members too.

Always act fairly and professionally when terminating somebody's employment contract. The person, not surprisingly, will likely be shocked and upset so you need to handle the situation with empathy while still being firm about your decision. Make sure you follow the legal procedures for your jurisdiction. Generally, you're entitled to let people go, but in many jurisdictions, you must follow a proper process in order to avoid legal issues.

When you let somebody go always explain to the remaining staff why you took the decision. Most of the time they are relieved at your decision. They usually know when somebody is not a good performer or a team player.

Over 20 years I dismissed very few people, but invariably after it happened one or more staff members would come to me and tell me that it was a good decision. They knew that the person wasn't right for the company.

LEGAL REQUIREMENTS

ESSENTIAL CONTRACTS

Every company needs some contracts and other legal documents to be able to run the business.

I'm not qualified to give definitive legal advice, but I can give you some guidance on the key documents you should put in place. However, I recommend that you get legal advice to ensure that you comply with local laws. Each jurisdiction will have its own legal requirements but here are some of the legal documents you will need. Many of these types of documents can be downloaded from the internet for a small outlay.

EMPLOYEE CONTRACTS

You need to make sure that you have contracts for employees. This is a legal requirement in most jurisdictions.

One important term you need to ensure you have covered regards intellectual property (IP). You must ensure that the company retains the IP to any work done by the employee while employed by you. Make sure you follow the rules and time limits for issuing the contracts to employees.

As you grow and acquire more staff, I recommend that you subscribe to an HR advisory service. They can help you with the management of staff contracts and ensure that they are kept up to date. They can also advise on disciplinary or termination matters.

EXTERNAL STAFF CONTRACTS

Any external staff (freelancers, consultants, outsourced organizations, etc.) should be signed to a contract. Never work with external people without having a contract in place.

Always work off your contractual terms for external staff. Don't let them impose their terms on you. If the external staff will be working on customer projects, then make sure you back-to-back any terms you are contracted to. In other words, if a customer has imposed certain terms on you then you should impose them on the external staff.

> *You must always protect your own, and your*
> *customers', intellectual property.*

Whenever possible, and within reason, try and match the payment terms you have with your customer(s) with your external staff.

You must protect ownership of your intellectual property when dealing with external staff. This must be included in the contract.

Even more important, you must protect your customer's intellectual property. So, if you're tied to some intellectual property restrictions by a customer, then you must make sure that anybody working on that account is also tied to the same terms.

You must ensure that the contract has a non-compete clause. You don't want to introduce external staff to your customers and then find that they've independently contracted to work directly with the customer.

You will also want to protect yourself from external organizations you work with hiring your employees.

NON-DISCLOSURE AGREEMENTS

You should have two types of Non-Disclosure Agreements (NDA)

1. One-way NDA
2. Mutual NDA

ONE-WAY NDA

Use this when you're prepared to enter into discussions with another party but you want to keep it confidential between you and them.

In most cases, it will be a customer or prospect who will ask you to sign an NDA before they will discuss a project with you.

NDAs are fairly standard agreements and generally not something to worry about. I rarely refused to sign one and I rarely had another organization refuse to sign one. If you do sign an NDA with another party, then make sure that all staff members know that you have signed it and that they should not break its terms.

MUTUAL NDA

Mutual NDAs are used when both you and another party could reveal things to each other. It protects either party if the other party breaks the confidentiality. If in doubt, it always looks professional if you suggest signing one before entering discussions.

TERMS & CONDITIONS

This is an important document that sets out your standard terms & conditions (T&Cs) for doing business with another party.

It's where you can lay down your payment terms, warranties, etc. It's always good to get your T&Cs in first before the other party waves theirs, but large corporations are more likely to insist on their terms as the base point for contractual discussions.

TIME RECORDING

TIMESHEETS

As previously mentioned, time recording is essential to a software development business, and a timesheet system is a key part of the infrastructure you should put in place.

I always referred to timesheets as the lifeblood of the organization. Without a timesheet system, I wouldn't have been able to invoice customers correctly.

When you have multiple people working on projects, and maybe in different locations, you can't keep track of all the hours expended unless you have some time recording system in place.

LOST BILLINGS HIT YOUR BOTTOM LINE

In our early days, I regularly found missed billings by cross-checking invoices with our timesheet system. This usually occurred because somebody hadn't completed their timesheet or there were gaps that they hadn't accounted for.

If we missed billing a customer, then it would have a direct effect on our bottom line and reduce our profits. That's why it's vital to capture all the time expended on projects. Put it another way, the customer is gaining from your sloppy procedures. Is that what you want?

TIMESHEETS ARE AN AUDIT TRAIL

Timesheets provide you with the evidence of work done if you need to justify your costs to a customer.

Many times over the years we were asked by a customer to provide some backup evidence for our billing. On some projects, you can provide evidence of deliverables but on other projects, you will need to provide evidence of time expended. And that's where a timesheet system is essential.

PROJECT ANALYTICS

Timesheets allow you to track resource usage on projects and to analyze how a project has performed compared to the original estimate. They allow you to better understand where projects have stalled or gone over budget. This can help you with future estimates particularly if you discover that you're consistently under-estimating certain activities.

You also need to be able to measure and manage bench time. Too much unscheduled bench time can decimate your profits, so this is one area you need to carefully control.

IMPLEMENTING A TIMESHEET SYSTEM

It starts at the top. As the business owner, you must set the standard for the company procedures. If you're doing billable work, then you must lead the way by consistently completing your timesheet on time.

Developers notoriously hate filling in timesheets, but you must ensure that it is part of their job. Talk about it during the induction and explain why it is so important to the company. Explain the benefits, such as quicker and more accurate billing, faster cash collection, more accurate estimates, etc. Make sure that they understand that it is not about spying or micro-management.

You must also ensure that any freelancers you use should also complete timesheets on your system. They will be a key part of a project, and you need to be able to analyze if it's profitable to continue using them.

Choose a cloud-based timesheet system ideally one with a mobile app as well.

Keep the data you require people to enter to a small set. The more data you try to capture the greater the resistance will be.

Establish a cut-off time for completion of timesheets, e.g. Monday morning by 10:00 am for the previous week.

Don't accept habitual lateness. If people are not completing their timesheets on time then this needs to be dealt with. Don't let it slide, otherwise you'll end up with incomplete data and you won't be able to bill customers on time.

CUSTOMER SERVICE

MAKE GREAT SERVICE YOUR MISSION

When I decided to set up my own company, I resolved to make excellence in customer service one of the things that would make us stand out. I knew from my previous experience that having long-term customers was one of the secrets to running a profitable business. I also knew that to retain customers for many years I would have to deliver great service.

> *"If you take the approach of earning your customers'*
> *business every day and treating them well, they're less*
> *likely to try someone else."*
>
> **Marilyn Suttle**

It's much easier to retain good customers than it is to find new ones, so you should put customer service at the core of your business.

Remember this: Customers pay your bills and enable you to be profitable and build a life of financial freedom—but only if you do good work and deliver great service.

BUILD A SERVICE CULTURE

You need to build a culture of service throughout your company. And it must start at the top with you.

Make it your goal to serve the hell out of your customers. If you make customer service your topmost priority, then this will attract more customers to you which in turn will lead to increased profitability.

You should become a lifelong student of customer service and continually be looking at ways you can improve the service you offer. Customer service is not one thing. It includes every interaction you have with a customer.

How do you answer the phone? Do you do that in a positive upbeat manner?

Do your people have a positive can-do attitude when talking to customers?

Do you honor your commitments to your customers?

How do you respond to customer requests? Do you get back to them asap?

Do you turn up on time to meet them?

And the big question: Do you go the extra mile at every opportunity?

CUSTOMER SERVICE TIPS

I made it my mission to learn as much as I could about delivering great customer service. Over the 20 years that I was CEO of my business, I was always thinking about ways to deliver better service. Here are some of the things I learned and implemented in my company.

UNDERPROMISE AND OVERDELIVER

Expectation management is the secret sauce of customer service. If you manage expectations correctly, then you will be perceived to have delivered better service than somebody who overpromises and fails to deliver as promised.

Underpromise doesn't mean setting low expectations. You must set the expectations high enough to ensure the customer will be happy but low enough so that you can exceed them if possible.

As an example, imagine the following two scenarios.

You take your car into a garage for a service and you ask when it will be ready. The service assistant says 2 pm. At 2 pm you go along, and your car isn't ready. You end up waiting until 3 pm for it. How happy are you? If you're like me, you wouldn't be very happy at all.

Alternatively, you take your car into a garage for a service. You're told the car will be ready at 4 pm. You happen to be passing the garage at 3 pm and you pop in to see how things are progressing. The service assistant tells you that your car is ready ahead of schedule. How happy are you now? Quite happy I'd imagine.

In both cases, the garage has delivered the same service. They've serviced your car and had it ready for 3 pm. But in one of these cases, your perception of the customer service is much greater than in the other.

Disney are the masters of this type of service. In their theme parks, they show the expected queuing time for each attraction. Have you ever noticed that the actual queuing time is never as long as the one shown at the entrance?

This is a deliberate policy of underpromising and overdelivering. They will always show a longer queuing time than they know will be the case so that you feel good when you get in earlier than you expected.

BE A POSITIVE, CAN-DO COMPANY

Over the years I learned that many internal IT departments are often regarded by the businesspeople as "No" people because they make everything seem so difficult or impossible to achieve.

We were often told by senior executives how easy it was to work with us because we always had a can-do attitude.

I used to coach my staff that they must never tell me, or a customer, that something can't be done.

Always respond positively. It's okay to say that it's more difficult, it will take longer, it is more expensive, or there's an alternative option. But don't say that it can't be done.

Customers want to work with companies that can get things done and they don't want to have to fight or argue to get it done. Make sure that your company operates with a can-do attitude. It will win you lots of repeat business from satisfied customers.

NEVER BAD-MOUTH CUSTOMERS OR COMPETITORS

If you bad-mouth other customers, what do you think a prospective customer will think? They're going to think that you'll eventually bad-mouth them.

And no matter how badly you want to beat your competitors to an opportunity the worst way to do that is to bad-mouth them. Far better to focus on your strengths and why you're a better choice than your competitors because when you bad-mouth other people you create bad vibes and you will make the customer suspicious that you would bad-mouth them also.

UNDERSTAND THE LIFETIME VALUE OF A CUSTOMER

Over a five- or ten-year period, a customer could be worth hundreds of thousands, even millions, of dollars to your business. And that doesn't include the additional value that can be gained from using a current customer to attract other new customers.

Understanding customer lifetime value will help inform your business strategy.

We had numerous customers that stayed with us for five years and more. Each of these customers was worth millions of dollars to us in lifetime value. In fact, some of these customers were worth north of ten million dollars to us.

So, instead of thinking about the value of a given deal or transaction, always think about the lifetime value of the customer. Let that drive your decisions when dealing with customers. Always make sure that you're offering the best service possible. That's how you build lifetime value.

BE AVAILABLE WHEN NEEDED

Give your best customers your cell phone number and tell them to call you at any time if ever there's an issue. This builds trust and shows your commitment to serving them.

In all the years that I did this, I was only called out-of-hours on about two occasions. Each time it was something that I personally, or one of my team, was able to help resolve.

Being available, and responding quickly in those urgent situations, earned us huge gratitude and kudos. And it helped us grow very profitable customer relationships.

LOOK AFTER YOUR CUSTOMERS

I regularly took customers out to lunch or dinner and I would pay for it. It was a way of saying thank you to them for the business they gave us. It was also a way to spend an hour or two in their company and to build a stronger relationship.

I would often get tickets to sports events or concerts and invite them to be my guest. I had some good customers who liked playing golf, so I would organize golf trips and invite them along. I took one customer to The Masters in Augusta one year. I also played golf with customers in various countries in Europe.

At Christmas, I would always buy expensive hampers and vintage wines for our customers. The higher up in the organization a person was the higher the value of wine or hamper they received.

But I had one golden rule when it came to looking after customers. I would only treat *existing* customers. I would never try to buy business from a prospect by treating them. That felt too close to bribery for me.

There is one caveat to this suggestion. You must always be aware of legal/compliance issues when spending money on customers. Some organizations prohibit their staff from taking gifts and/or accepting invitations to meals, events, etc.

REMEMBER PERSONAL DETAILS ABOUT THEM

Each time you engage with a prospect or customer it's a chance to learn something new about them. Make it your goal to find out things about them in a casual and unobtrusive way. Ask about their partner/spouse and/or their kids and remember their names.

Ask about their holiday plans, their hobbies and activities, etc. Engage with them when you have overlapping interests.

Remembering this stuff helps build rapport when you next engage with them. Keep track of the information you learn in a CRM system so you won't forget it and also share it with others on your team.

With all my long-term customers I built a great rapport with them because I could discuss topics that I knew would interest them. I could also mention their wives and kids by name and check up on how they were doing. As I mentioned previously, some of my best customers became friends of mine because we found common ground or interests that we shared.

DON'T GO INTO BATTLE OVER MINOR THINGS

There will be times when the customer might be insistent or stubborn about a particular point and you may be confident or even certain that they are wrong. Sometimes, when it's a minor matter with a low impact, it's better to give way and keep them as a satisfied customer.

The customer may not always be right but they are
always the customer

You don't have to win every dispute or disagreement with a customer to be a good leader. Far better to look at the potential lifetime value of the customer and choose to back off occasionally.

QUALITY

ALWAYS DELIVER GREAT WORK

Fundamental to offering a great service is the quality of work you deliver. Your business will not survive if the quality of your work is consistently poor.

The only work worth doing is great work

Poor quality work will impact your business in many ways including

- It will kill your profitability
- You will lose repeat customers
- You will lose recurring revenue
- You will not get referrals
- You will lose your reputation
- Ultimately you will lose your business

BUILD A QUALITY CULTURE

You must make sure that you build a quality culture in your business and that starts at the top with you.

You must set high standards for what's acceptable quality. But at the same time, you have to know when to deliver.

Pursuing perfection is admirable, but you also must know when the software is good enough to ship.

DON'T ACCEPT POOR WORK

As a small business, you can't afford to carry people who consistently deliver poor work.

Poor developers will damage your reputation and your business. They are usually difficult to manage, and they leave a trail of issues behind them for other developers to mop up. If you find you've hired a poor developer, then don't carry them out of a sense of loyalty. That loyalty could bring your business down.

SCALING YOUR TEAM

HOW TO SCALE YOUR TEAM

One of the biggest challenges in trying to grow your business is knowing how and when to scale your team. Getting this right is one of the keys to success.

As I previously mentioned, controlling your costs and bench time is essential if you're going to run a profitable business, so deciding to hire more staff is critical to the future of the business.

You won't be able to grow your business to seven figures and more without hiring staff. You won't win big, lucrative projects if you don't scale your team. I used a combination of these resourcing strategies to scale through multiple levels of growth:

- Employees
- Freelancers
- Offshore resources
- Partners
- Graduates

EMPLOYEES

Your employees are the bedrock of your business. They will hopefully stay with you for years and play a key part in the growth of your business.

You need to hire employees if you want to build a trusted team of lieutenants who you can delegate work to. You also need employees who buy into your vision and who have a loyalty to the business if you are going to get to seven figures.

However, hiring employees is not something that can be taken lightly. You need to be certain that you will have enough work and enough revenue coming in so that you can keep them busy and can pay them every month.

It's very much a step-by-step process when hiring employees. Win some work, hire some people. Win some more work, hire some more people. At the same time, you are mixing the hiring of employees with the other strategies below.

FREELANCERS

Using freelancers is the quickest way to scale when you win a new project because you only need to hire them for the duration of the project. However, there are pros and cons to using freelancers.

FREELANCERS: PROS

1. You can usually hire freelancers quickly. You can wait until the project is secured before hiring anybody.

2. You can hire the specific experience needed for the job.

3. You don't need to deal with employee contracts, health benefits, etc.

4. You hire them for the job and then they go.

5. They don't have an ongoing cost once the job is complete.

FREELANCERS: CONS

1. They are guns for hire. They are there to earn money with no sense of loyalty or buy-in to your long-term vision.

2. They are expensive. Your margins could be lower.

3. They can be difficult to manage and to get to work to your standards.

4. You often won't know the quality of their work until they are gone.

5. They won't be around to fix problems and provide ongoing support.

6. You must watch out for potential tax implications if they stay working for you.

TIPS FOR HIRING FREELANCERS

1. Check samples of their code quality. Get them to walk you through some code they've written so you can see the level of work they're capable of.

2. Make sure that you get references and then follow them up. This is essential. Speak to some of their previous employers. You don't want to discover later that they leave a trail of bad code behind them.

3. Keep them focused by being very clear about the scope of the task you're hiring them for. Make sure they understand the commitments and deadlines you've agreed with your customer.

4. Get them under contract and make sure that you protect your IP and the IP of your customers.

OFFSHORE RESOURCES

I used offshore resources for more than 20 years to help us scale at each stage of our business. It enabled me to grow the business quickly and cost-effectively.

I learned a lot of things about working with offshore resources. Here are the pros and cons.

OFFSHORE RESOURCES: PROS

1. If you line up things in advance you can build a team quickly from scratch.

2. You can take on much bigger projects than you otherwise could do.

3. The quality of work can be very good. I've worked with some amazing offshore developers.

4. The costs can be low, and the profit margins can be very high.

5. You can often turn the work on and off as required so you don't carry the costs or have bench time.

OFFSHORE RESOURCES: CONS

1. Managing remote people/teams can be difficult.

2. There can be time zone, language, and cultural issues.

3. Lack of visibility of what's happening.

4. Lack of control if the project starts slipping.

5. The quality of work can be poor. I dealt with some poor developers in our early days until we got better at working with offshore resources.

OFFSHORE RESOURCES: TIPS

1. Build relationships with offshore companies in advance. Get to know the company and some of the people you

might work with. That way you can be ready to quickly take on a new project.

2. Give them non-critical jobs at first until you see how they work.

3. Get them working on black box tasks as much as possible.

4. Keep command and control at your headquarters. Never hand over control of a project to an offshore company.

5. Make sure that you have a tight contract with them so that they can't poach your customers or your staff.

6. Communicate, communicate, communicate. Never let them go dark on you. That's how things go wrong.

7. Make sure the time zone works for you. Is there enough overlap in working hours so that you can talk to them each day?

8. Get them on a week-long sale or return basis. I always applied my risk-reversal technique to offshore companies. I would get them to agree that when they assigned somebody new to us we would have a week to validate their skills. If the developer wasn't acceptable to us, then we wouldn't pay for that week. If we kept the developer, then we would pay for the week and would continue to pay from that point on. This put the onus on them to make sure that they provided us with good people.

9. Bring them onshore if feasible. This won't always be possible, but as we grew, I would quite often fly some of the offshore team to our offices for one to four weeks so that we could get to know them and build a good

relationship with them. We also got the chance to see how they worked and to transfer our knowledge and skills and quality culture to them.

WHERE TO FIND OFFSHORE RESOURCES

I've worked with people in various locations around the world, and I've had good and bad experiences in each country that I've hired from.

The Philippines has many English speakers and the cost base is very attractive. They generally have a good work ethic. However, the infrastructure is not as good as in the West and I've lost contact with people for days because of tropical storms.

Brazil has a growing population of software developers who speak good English. I've not experienced any significant infrastructure or connectivity issues. I visited there to see an offshore center and was impressed with how modern the set-up was. An advantage of Brazil for U.S. businesses is that there is a much smaller time difference than with other parts of the world.

We used developers from Romania for most of the 20 years that I was CEO. We mostly had very good experiences with them and we experienced very few connection problems. Romania has an excellent hi-tech education system and culturally they're more aligned with western standards. They are incredibly talented and they all speak excellent English. The costs in Romania have risen in recent years but they are still cost-effective when compared to most other western companies. Other European countries with a good pool of developers and low costs include Bulgaria, Ukraine, and Belarus.

Over the years we worked with various Indian outsourcing companies but had mixed results. We eventually set up our own office in Chennai and this enabled us to provide a 24x7 support service to our large customers.

PARTNERSHIPS

Partnerships allow you to supplement your resource pool and/or to take on work that you might not otherwise have the skills to do.

Over the years, we partnered with many companies that had complementary skills such as UX design, infrastructure expertise, development skills, etc. These partnerships enabled us to take on bigger projects that required multiple skills. They also gave us access to additional development resources to help us grow our business without incurring the full-time cost.

Even before we landed any new customers, I had meetings with potential partners so that I knew if an opportunity came our way I could call on additional help. Begin by building a network of people in your area that you could call on if necessary. Arrange to meet some local companies or consultancies over coffee or lunch and start building relationships.

A side benefit to this approach is that you might also be asked to help one of these partners on one of their projects. Here are some pros and cons of dealing with partners.

PARTNERSHIPS: PROS

1. You can take on bigger projects requiring a range of skills.

2. You can generally scale up quickly.

3. You can scale without taking on additional fixed costs.

4. You can generally scale down very quickly to reduce costs.

PARTNERSHIPS: CONS

1. Partners have their own business to run, so you may not always get their best people.

2. Other projects they win could put pressure on them to pull people out of your project.

3. They will want to earn their usual day rates, which means your profit margins will be very thin.

PARTNERSHIPS: TIPS

1. Build relationships at the executive level. Meet with the owners or principals of the business to make sure that they're a company you'd be happy to work with.

2. Make sure your core values are aligned. If your core values are fundamentally different, then the relationship won't last.

3. Agree on rates and margins that are needed by both sides. Try to get a discount off their normal rates, as you will be bringing additional business to them.

4. Expect to give them a discount on your rates if they bring business to you.

5. Get mutual NDAs in place when discussing opportunities. Don't mention prospect names and other details before you have an agreement in place.

6. Make sure partners are on back-to-back agreements. If you are tied to certain conditions on a project you will need to ensure that the partner is also tied into those conditions if they work for you.

GRADUATES

Over the years I gave many graduates their first job in IT. They can often supplement experienced people and provide extra capability within teams. They can be a good way to grow your resource pool, but you mustn't rely solely on graduates. You will always need good experienced people. Here are some pros and cons of hiring graduates.

GRADUATES: PROS

1. They are low cost and allow you to balance your project costs.

2. They are usually very keen and eager to learn. Generally, they are not know-it-alls and are easy to work with.

3. Good graduates can be very smart and quick learners. They can be valuable additions to your team.

4. They will often take on the work that more experienced developers hate doing.

GRADUATES: CONS

1. They are inexperienced and may disrupt the progress of the team.

2. You need to give them time to progress and to learn.

3. They will make mistakes.

4. You can't have a lot of graduates. I had a max of two new graduates at any time.

HIRING BUSINESSPEOPLE

As you grow through six figures and on to seven figures you will need to hire non-technical people. For example, you will need bookkeepers, marketers, and salespeople.

BOOKKEEPING

In the very early days of the business, you will likely do this yourself or you might even get your spouse or life partner to help. You also have the option to outsource bookkeeping through a site such as Fiverr.

However, as your business grows proper bookkeeping will become even more important. You need to watch out for the crossover point where the number of invoices and staff grow, and the bookkeeping workload grows. The management of timesheets, generation of invoices, chasing payment, paying suppliers, etc., will become a burden unless somebody is dedicated to the task.

As I've said previously, getting invoices sent out on time and collecting payment on time is vital to your cash flow and the overall sustainability of the business, so you can't afford to let these tasks slide.

At the earliest point possible you need to hire somebody to take charge of the administration and bookkeeping functions. You should not try to run this yourself. Your job is to manage it, *not* to do it. You probably won't even need a full-time person to do the job. You could easily grow to seven figures with a part-time bookkeeper.

MARKETING

Marketing is the single most important function that you need to ensure continuity through all stages of growth. Don't make the mistake of curtailing marketing when you get busy. I did that and regretted it! We got so busy in the early days that we took our eyes off the marketing. We subsequently found ourselves with periods of bench time when some projects ended because we hadn't kept our marketing efforts going.

In the early days, you might have to take on some marketing activities yourself until you start generating cash. Even then you should try and outsource anything you can through an outsourcing site. Once you're generating steady cash you should then look at hiring a part-time marketing assistant to ensure that you're constantly creating new opportunities.

SALES

To grow to seven figures and beyond you will need a dedicated sales resource to keep chasing and working new opportunities.

The world is full of bad salespeople.

If you've partnered with a salesperson this will be easier to manage, otherwise you will have to consider hiring a salesperson. Finding good salespeople is one of the hardest parts of growing a business. Unfortunately, there are many poor salespeople out there. Finding good ones is difficult and time-consuming. My strongest advice is that you should make sure that you hire somebody who has worked for a services business and not a product business.

Product salespeople are usually very poor at selling services. They find it difficult to sell something intangible—services, compared to selling something tangible—products.

Make sure any salespeople you hire are compatible with your core values, otherwise you will have huge cultural issues to deal with. You don't want to hire somebody who sells in a sleazy or aggressive way. That will kill your reputation and cost you business.

Also, make sure that they are comfortable with your core story. Walk them through the core story when you've shortlisted them and make sure that they will buy into your vision.

You should only hire people who have a proven track record in selling six- and seven-figure deals. If they've only ever sold small deals, they will struggle with pricing larger deals and will be inclined to offer discounts to get the price down.

In the ideal world, you would look to hire somebody you know to be good. Maybe you know somebody who is working for another company and who is successful at selling.

There is one golden rule about hiring salespeople. You must always get references and you must *always* follow them up. Good salespeople are adept at selling themselves. They can talk themselves up and tell good stories. Most are good at projecting themselves as likable people. But can they sell?

The best way to get the answer to that is to check the facts about any deals they claim to have sold and, most importantly, speak to past employers. One key question to ask in interviews is "What was your role in that?" Salespeople will often talk about big deals they landed. However, many big projects need a team of people to win the deal. Make sure that the person you're interviewing was the lead person who made the deal happen.

STRATEGIC ALLIANCES

Strategic alliances are one of the most important growth hacks for a small company.

> *"If you can learn to stand on the shoulders of giants, you can get bigger, faster"*

Isaac Newton

There are a number of different types of alliances you can build.

VENDOR ALLIANCES

Vendor alliances are typically set up with large companies where you work with their platform or solutions to go to market.

Often you will need to be certified in their technology in order to take advantage of the alliance. Examples can include Microsoft, Oracle, IBM, Amazon, Salesforce, SAP, etc., etc.

Here are some pros and cons of working with vendors.

VENDOR ALLIANCES: PROS

1. They typically have a huge market share and could introduce you to many opportunities.

2. They give you credibility, particularly if you're certified in their technology.

3. The vendor can introduce you to other market sectors that you might not otherwise have access to.

4. You are more likely to find big deals through a vendor. Even one big deal could significantly grow your business.

5. Enterprise-class platforms attract big licenses and services. Services can often be five times the license value or more.

6. You could end up being a partner for many years so the benefits could be significant over time.

VENDOR ALLIANCES: CONS

1. You will usually be a small fish in a big pond. You'll be competing for business against many other companies unless you're involved in the early stages of a new product.
2. The vendor only cares about their numbers. If you're not helping them hit their numbers, then you're toast.
3. Some vendors have been known to bully small companies if a deal becomes successful. They can put pressure on your rates and even take work back from you or give it to another company.
4. There can be cultural issues between you and the vendor that can make it difficult to deal with them.
5. They can put a lot of demands on you and consume lots of your time for little return.
6. There are usually costs involved in signing up as an alliance partner and/or becoming certified in their technology.
7. You will usually have to hit certain targets to stay as an alliance partner.
8. They can change the rules of the alliance at any time. If you're reliant on them, then this could be very damaging.

MANAGEMENT CONSULTANCIES

Consulting partners can include management consultancies, specialist business consulting organizations, etc. Many of these companies already work with partners and regularly are looking for additional partners to fill in gaps in their experience and capabilities.

You should be looking to build consulting partnerships right from the get-go, as they can be a quick way to get business, particularly if you have skills in an in-demand area.

MANAGEMENT CONSULTANCIES: PROS

1. They can help you plug gaps in your skills, and you can do the same for them.

2. They can allow you to offer a full solution to customers.

3. The partner can introduce you to other market sectors that you might not otherwise have access to.

4. Partners who work upstream at board level will know about projects long before the customer starts procuring services.

5. They can very quickly introduce you to new business with some of their existing customers.

6. A good partnership can last for years and be mutually rewarding to both parties.

MANAGEMENT CONSULTANCIES: CONS

1. Often, they will want to "own" the customer. You will, therefore, have to work on their terms.

2. You may have to put in pre-sales time with them for free.

3. There can be cultural issues between both parties that can make it difficult to work with them.

4. They have their business to run and won't always be focused on helping you or working with you.

TIPS FOR STRATEGIC ALLIANCES

The best way to build strategic alliances is to approach a company and tell them what you're going to do for them.

Ask not what your strategic partner can do for you, but what you can do for the partnership.

If you start by telling them what you want from the alliance, then you are less likely to gain their attention. Focus first on what you bring to the deal and how that can help them build *their* business.

Can you offer them a competitive advantage, faster time to market, skills they don't have, etc.? Can you give them access to customers or markets they don't currently have access to?

Having a great core story will significantly help you when approaching potential alliance partners. It will be much easier for them to understand what your unique offering is and how it could help them.

If they can see how you can help them grow their business, then they are more likely to be interested in helping you grow yours. They may even ask you to present your core story to some of their existing customers.

With management consultancies, it's a good idea to look for symbiotic relationships where your joint skills complement each other. The best results generally occur where the parties are not competing with each other in the marketplace.

With consulting partners, you should build relationships at the senior level. You should make sure there's a cultural fit between both parties. The better the fit the more stable the relationship is likely to be.

Vendor partners usually operate more programmatically. You won't generally get access to the topmost level of the organization. You will normally be assigned to a program manager.

I would advise against putting all your eggs in the one basket and relying solely on an alliance partner to bring you all your business. A single partner could turn off the tap at any time and leave you high and dry.

Always make sure that you have mutual NDAs in place when dealing with strategic partners. Never discuss customers' or prospects' names with them without having an agreement in place.

And finally, make sure to deliver excellence in service when working with an alliance partner. Otherwise, the partnership won't last.

REPEAT CUSTOMERS

THREE WAYS TO GROW A BUSINESS

U.S. marketing guru, Jay Abraham, says that there are only three ways to grow a business:

1. Increase the number of customers you have. Get more new prospects and turn them into paying customers.

2. Increase the frequency customers buy from you. Get each customer to buy from you more often.

3. Increase the average transaction value. Get each customer to buy more at each purchase.

We've already looked at how you can attract new customers. Now we'll look at how you can get them to buy more often from you.

CULTIVATE REPEAT CUSTOMERS

You need relatively few customers to get to seven figures—as long as you can get existing customers to buy more often from you.

The holy grail of your business should be to have customers buying your services for many years ahead. It is *far* easier to get customers to buy more often from you than to find new customers, so make sure you serve the hell out of existing customers.

According to research done by Bain & Company, it costs six to seven times more money to land a new customer than to retain an existing one.

According to Marketing Metrics, the probability of selling to an existing customer is 60–70 percent. The probability of selling to a new prospect is only 5–20 percent! And a huge advantage of repeat business that is often overlooked is that you don't usually have to compete for it. You get offered repeat business because the customer already knows you and trusts you and they don't offer the work to other companies. To get repeat business you must ensure that you:

1. Deliver top-quality work

2. Meet your commitments: be reliable

3. Fix problems quickly when they arise

4. Go the extra mile: regularly over-deliver

5. Are perceived as easy to work with

6. Continually build rapport with key decision-makers

7. Are honest and fair in your dealings with them

TIPS FOR WINNING REPEAT CUSTOMERS

Work onsite whenever you can. This exposes you and your team to the customer's staff thereby enabling you to build relationships with a whole range of people.

Always be alert to other opportunities to help your customers. When working onsite you'll often hear about other work or projects they need help with. Don't be afraid to volunteer to help or to take on another project. Make sure to coach your staff to be alert for other opportunities and to report them back to you if they hear something.

Stay in touch with your customers even if you're not currently working with them. Keep them updated on your latest work/projects by sending them emails or newsletters.

Stay in regular contact with current and past customers.
Time spent with them over coffee or lunch is always a
good investment.

Take customers out for coffee or lunch/dinner to catch up and to continually develop the relationship. Thank them for their business and let them know you appreciate it.

Remember special occasions birthdays, milestone anniversaries, etc. Write them a note of congratulations if you know they've had a new baby. Congratulate them on a promotion or new job title.

If one of your contacts leaves your customer's organization, then congratulate them on their new job. Arrange to go and see them over coffee or lunch. If they can recommend you to their new employer, then you can quickly win a new customer. We landed one of our biggest customers this way.

Invite customers to events/webinars, etc., you are holding. They won't always be able to attend, but they will appreciate the invitation.

Send them articles that you think they might be interested in. Watch for trends in their industry and comment on them from a perspective that they would be interested in.

Publish valuable content that they would be interested in. The more that this content relates to them and their industry the more interesting it will be for them. Always be ready to make suggestions to them. Here are some:

- Suggest ways that they could use new technology.
- Suggest ways that could save them money.
- Suggest improvements in their processes that you could help with

The bottom line is that your existing customers are like a gold mine that will keep producing gold for many years. As long as you do good work, deliver great service, and generally look after them you will get to seven figures far quicker than by continually having to find new customers.

RECURRING REVENUE

THE POWER OF RECURRING REVENUE

One of your primary business goals should be to secure as much recurring revenue as possible.

If you can ensure a certain level of recurring revenues and manage associated operating expenses, then you give yourself a cushion of financial security over a longer period.

Recurring revenue indicates that your business is providing a service that is needed and valued. It's a validation that you have a sustainable business model and makes your business much more attractive to investors and acquirers.

> *"Recurring revenue is the portion of a company's revenue that is expected to continue in the future. Unlike one-off sales, these revenues are predictable, stable, and can be counted on to occur at regular intervals going forward with a relatively high degree of certainty."*

Investopedia

BENEFITS OF RECURRING REVENUE

There are many benefits of recurring revenue. Here are some:

- Predictable cash flow. We had seven-figure recurring revenues each year which made our business very stable.
- You can get paid in advance, so your cash reserves are always healthy. You then have the comfort of knowing that you can pay your staff and your bills.
- You can remove seasonal variations in income, and you can plan many months in advance.
- It secures a long-term relationship with the customer. You can then easily sell them additional services.
- It can be very profitable as you have no sales costs.

- It will also add significant value to your company. Investors and acquirers love dealing with companies that have recurring income.

TYPES OF RECURRING REVENUE

There are several types of recurring revenue that are relevant to a software development business. These include:

- Pay-for-work retainer
- Pay-for-access retainer
- Done-for-you services
- Support contracts
- License fees
- Commissions

PAY-FOR-WORK RETAINER

This is where the customer will pay you a monthly fee to carry out some work. They won't always know what the exact work is, but they will expect to have a number of tasks for you to do.

We had a pay-for-work retainer with one customer who guaranteed us a minimum income each month. However, we also had to be able to take on extra work as demand increased.

PAY-FOR-ACCESS RETAINER

This is where the customers will pay you a monthly fee to have access to your knowledge.

This type of retainer is more applicable to consulting services rather than development services. However, as you grow your business and take on additional skills, you may find opportunities to sell consulting services under a retainer agreement.

DONE-FOR-YOU SERVICES

If you've followed my earlier advice, then you should have some done-for-you services in your portfolio. You should aim to get these done-for-you services contracted on a recurring basis. Look for ways that you could bill for them on a monthly/quarterly/annual basis.

SUPPORT CONTRACTS

Support contracts were one of the most important revenue sources in our business.

After we landed some large projects, we then started each subsequent year with more than $1m in pre-signed support contracts. That was great for our cash flow, as these contracts were usually paid annually in advance, with some of them paid quarterly.

We sold support contracts with nearly all of our development projects. They acted as insurance for our customers, as they knew that we would fix and support the system at any time during its life.

Our biggest contracts were typically for 5- to 10-year terms, which gave us great predictability. Other smaller contracts would be for one year and upwards. Each contract would automatically renew unless we were given advance notice of cancellation.

Typically, support contracts are charged at 20% of the project cost. However, you could negotiate a lower rate for a longer contract term.

Support contracts can be very profitable, as you may be able to cover much of the support from your existing resource pool. Over time, as you sign more contracts, you can add some dedicated support staff while still maintaining good margins on the work.

As systems mature support calls reduce—but the fee stays the same each year. So you end up with less work to do for the same fee.

LICENSE FEES

There are typically two sources of license fees you can generate.
- Licenses of your own software
- Licenses of a third-party vendor's software

If you create a product or some other intellectual property, then you can drive license-fee revenue. The more that you can make this recurring or subscription-based revenue the better.

You can also derive recurring revenue from vendor licenses that you sell or influence. Typically this is where you have a partnership with a vendor that rewards you with a percentage of the license fees.

These arrangements usually attract a 25% to 40% share of the license fee revenue. And if the license fee is a recurring one, then you can expect to get ongoing revenue from it.

WAYS TO SECURE RECURRING REVENUE

RETAINERS

I generally advise against trying to sell retainers to new customers, unless they specifically ask for it. It's a hard sell and can look a bit pushy if you try to sell a retainer when they don't know you well.

It's much easier to agree to a retainer when the customer has seen the quality of your work and can see the value of paying you a retainer. If you can show them a six-month plan (or more) for how your services might be used, then it's much easier to have a conversation about a retainer.

When agreeing to a retainer you should always bill in advance. If you can get an annual retainer billed in advance, then you've hit gold but be prepared to accept quarterly or six-monthly billing, as these are still good alternatives.

Make sure that they must give you at least 30 days advance notice if they intend to cancel the retainer agreement. Try hard to avoid tying the service to one person. You need to retain the flexibility to use different resources to fulfill the service. This might not always be possible, as the customer may want a particular individual in which case you may have to accept this.

Avoid carry-overs if you can. In other words, if the agreement states that they commit to using a certain number of days in a period and they don't use all of these days, then they can't carry them over to the next period. The reason for this is that they could land you with a resourcing issue if they carry lots of days over.

However, be careful when negotiating the agreement that you don't negotiate too hard on this to the point where the customer is unwilling to sign a retainer agreement. I would sometimes compromise and allow a customer to carry over a small number of days per period just to ensure we reached an amicable agreement.

Ensure that you have a mechanism to increase the charge if the work scales. This often happens with retainer work. The workload increases as you work with them, so you need to make sure that the agreement allows you to bill more.

Retainers are very valuable for your business so make sure you deliver value and over-deliver where you can. This will increase your chances of the customer renewing the retainer agreement.

SUPPORT CONTRACTS

Always aim to ask the customer if they will need a support contract as part of the project discussions. You don't get what you don't ask for.

Most large projects will require you to offer ongoing support and maintenance. Aim to charge 20% of the project value, but you can afford to yield to 15% in order to secure a contract. You could even accept a bit less for a long-term contract. On larger projects, I would aim for a five-year term as a minimum. The more critical the system is the more likely the customer will want to secure long-term support.

One of the terms of the agreement should be to allow you to have an annual inflationary uplift included. You should also have a term that allows you to uplift the cost of support if you make major additions to the system.

> *Support contracts are extremely valuable to your*
> *business, so make sure that you deliver on the contract*
> *commitments.*

Typical contracts will have P1, P2, P3 priority requirements. Get all hands on deck when you get a P1 issue and make sure that you fix it as fast as possible.

Most of our contracts were based on offering second level support so we only got called when the first level support team couldn't resolve the issue.

You can also add in uplifts for out-of-hours support or support for different time zones. This can be another profitable addition to the recurring revenue.

CREATING INTELLECTUAL PROPERTY

ADDING VALUE TO YOUR BUSINESS

Even though you're running a services business you should always be looking for opportunities to create intellectual property (IP). The benefits of owning intellectual property can include:

- Differentiation and competitive advantage
- Higher margins are possible
- As a loss-leader, it can win you business
- You can generate recurring license revenue
- It can increase the value of your company

TYPES OF INTELLECTUAL PROPERTY

There are numerous ways to add intellectual property to your portfolio. These include:

- Unique processes you use
- Publications or content you create
- Frameworks or libraries you build
- Products or apps you develop
- Add-on modules for third-party party software

UNIQUE PROCESSES YOU USE

Have you got special techniques or skills and/or a unique approach to how you do something? If you have, you could document your processes and package them as a specialized offering that is only available from you. The more the process is focused on your chosen niche the more valuable it becomes.

Make sure that you give this unique process a brand name. This will make it seem more like a product offering and will make it more attractive to prospects. In any conversations internally with your staff, or externally with prospects and customers, you should refer to the process by its brand name. This will strengthen the perception of it as a packaged piece of intellectual copyright.

PUBLICATIONS OR CONTENT

Creating unique content is a great way to build up your IP. There are many ways to do this including:

- Writing white papers/research reports
- Writing eBooks on a relevant topic
- Publishing a book
- Creating automated webinars
- Creating SlideShare presentations
- Publishing how-to videos
- Delivering an online course
- Running a podcast

Each piece of content is unique to you and can help build your authority and differentiate you from competitors.

FRAMEWORKS OR LIBRARIES

Over the years of running my business, we built a number of frameworks that were invaluable for winning new business. The first one I built was an intranet framework that led to more than seven figures in license and services revenue.

We also built libraries of code to solve specific problems and to speed up development, reduce risk & cost, etc. Each of these libraries and frameworks was given a brand name and we would make a big play of their advantages when talking to prospects and customers.

ADD-ONS FOR THIRD-PARTY SOFTWARE

There is often a valuable market in building add-ons or extensions for established products or platforms.

Major enterprise platforms such as Salesforce, SAP, Dynamics CRM, etc., have huge user bases. If you build add-ons to platforms like these, then you could have a valuable piece of IP on your hands and it could open up many opportunities for you.

You could also build add-ons or extensions for operating systems like Windows or Linux or cloud platforms such as Azure, AWS, etc.

These add-ons or extensions can help you win new customers and new projects and can drive significant service revenue your way.

PRODUCTS OR APPS YOU DEVELOP

As you grow your services business you will encounter opportunities to develop products or apps.

You might work with a customer where you undertake a project for them to develop a system that you realize has commercial value in the same, or other, markets.

You could negotiate with the customer to acquire the IP or rights to resell the product or app. I've done this several times over the years.

Alternatively, you may spot an opportunity to develop a product in a niche and you could get one or more customers to pre-commit to buying the product. A good product or app could be transformative for your business as it can create additional revenue and increase your value.

You could license it on an annual/subscription basis to generate recurring revenues and/or you could use the product as a loss leader to increase your services revenue.

If the product is an enterprise-class product, then it can pull in many times the license revenue in services revenue. From my own experience, I can testify that good products can generate 5–10 times the license costs in services revenue.

A good product could be a game-changer for your business. But don't underestimate how difficult it is to pivot and become a product company.

Having a good product in your portfolio can be a very valuable asset to your business. It can multiply your value and make you more attractive as an acquisition target. But it's not without its challenges.

You may be faced with the dilemma of whether to stay as a services business or become a product business. It's easy to get hooked on the idea of building products but very few products ever succeed and cover their costs. A product company is a different shape to a services business. *Do not* underestimate how hard it is to achieve that.

It's one thing to have a product or two in your services portfolio, but it's a different thing to pivot and become 100% product focused. It's not impossible, as many companies have managed to do it, but it isn't easy, and you will have to reshape the company and create a different structure with different roles.

If you've already got some customers using your product, and you're certain there is a good market for it, then pivoting to become a product company could be a game-changer for you. Be aware though that you may also need funding to grow quickly before you get overtaken by a competitor with greater funding.

ADDING PILLARS

THE PARTHENON PHILOSOPHY

One of the most powerful marketing concepts I've ever encountered is The Parthenon Philosophy. I learned this from U.S. marketing guru Jay Abraham.

The Greek Parthenon in Athens is a building that has stood for thousands of years, surviving earthquakes, fires, explosions, weather extremes, etc. Its strength lies in the fact that it is composed of multiple pillars with no single weak point of failure. Most businesses only use one primary method (or pillar) for bringing in customers. If that method collapses or fails, they go out of business.

However, if you use the Parthenon Philosophy and have more than one source of revenue (or pillar), you can strengthen your business, and make it more resistant to shocks.

Are there other services that you could help your ideal customers with?

Are there other services that could attract a different type of customer?

Are there synergistic services that could drive revenue to your main business?

Examples of other pillars you could add could include:

- Additional language/database offerings
- Third-party product implementation and support services
- DevOps consulting
- Agile coaching/consulting
- Strategy Consulting
- Training
- Testing/QA
- Additional partner/alliance relationships

A good example of an additional pillar we added to our business was a CRM practice. We were doing a lot of development for some large companies and we noticed that they were all investing heavily in CRM systems. So we set up a separate CRM team within our business and we started offering CRM implementation and support services.

One new pillar in your business could bring in an
additional seven figures in revenue

This led to us winning significant business from existing customers as well as attracting a range of new customers.

We also noticed that investment in CRM systems was consistent over the long term as companies were constantly looking at different ways to grow customer relationships. By adding this additional pillar to our business, we brought in millions of dollars of additional revenues.

So, always be looking to add new pillars that can bring in additional revenues and provide greater stability, and growth opportunities, for your business.

EVENTS, WEBINARS, AND SPEAKING

There are many ways to attract new customers. One of the best ways is to put yourself out there in front of your ideal customers by hosting events or webinars or by speaking at public events.

HOSTING EVENTS

If you've got a great core story and a well-defined niche, then you could run an event for an invited audience of your ideal customers.

A great format is the breakfast briefing, held in a location convenient to your audience. (You could also try an early evening cocktail event.)

If you hold a short (less than two hours) briefing on a specific topic of interest to your intended audience, you get the chance to build your credibility and impress your ideal customers. Remember that even if you just get one customer from an event it will pay you back many times the cost of the event.

We held many events where we attracted from 6 to 30 key people. Sometimes we signed up a new customer or won more business from an existing customer.

I remember the first event we held. I was as nervous as hell as we hadn't done one before. I kept imagining all the things that could go wrong. My biggest worry was that nobody would turn up on the day.

But about 20 people attended the event and we signed up a major new customer on the back of the event. That customer went on to spend hundreds of thousands of dollars with us. From that point on I was a fan of hosting events.

TIPS FOR HOSTING EVENTS

If you plan to base your event around your core story, then don't present your whole story. Present a subset of it or use a specific focus area. Reserve presenting the whole core story for one-to-one scenarios with a prospect.

It's always a good idea to show a demo of something that would appeal to your audience. It's a great way to vary the content of your event.

Alternatively, or in addition, if you can show a video that supports your presentation, then that will increase the interest level of your presentation.

> *Getting one of your customers to speak at your event will greatly increase the appeal to others in the same industry.*

If you can get an existing customer to speak at your event, you will enhance the value of the event significantly. Other businesses will be interested in hearing from somebody with similar challenges to theirs.

If you have signed up as an alliance partner with a major vendor, then you should try and get one of the vendor's people to present at your event. Most vendors are usually willing to provide somebody to speak if they know that some ideal customers will be attending.

At the end of your presentation hold a Q&A session. This is a great way to engage with your prospects and to show your expertise.

Most important, you must have a Call to Action (CTA) at the end of the event. You must give the prospect the next step to take.

You can use this opportunity to give a special on-the-day-only discount for one of your productized offerings. As an example, if they sign up then and there, they get a 50% discount off your done-for-you service.

HOSTING WEBINARS

You can easily create a webinar from some key elements of your core story and then present it and/or pre-record it for replay.

Ideally, you would want to host it live so that you can engage with your audience, but you can get a long tail of use from it by recording it as well.

With a live webinar, you get the big advantage of hosting a live Q&A session at the end of the webinar. With a pre-recorded webinar you can set it up to play at times convenient for your audience. You could use products such as Stealth Seminar or EverWebinar to host it. They both offer just-in-time capabilities.

One of the most powerful ways of running a successful webinar is to co-host it with somebody who already has an established following. You could co-host with a social media influencer, author, podcast host, industry thought leader, alliance partner, etc. Once you open your mind to collaborating you open the door to lots of possibilities.

WEBINAR HOSTING TIPS

A webinar is a window into your organization, so make sure that you do it professionally. Make sure that you have a quality presentation to run through.

With a pre-recorded webinar you can record a professional voiceover if you're not comfortable doing it. You can use a site such as Fiverr to find somebody with a great presenting voice.

Keep it to about 45 minutes max. Longer than that and the audience's attention begins to drop off.

If you record a live webinar then make sure that you include the Q&A session as part of the recording. Hearing other people's questions answered is a valuable part of the webinar.

There is one other alternative to consider. You can deliver a pre-recorded webinar and then go live for the Q&A session. So, the first 45 minutes are pre-recorded but then you take questions while people are still connected.

SPEAKING ENGAGEMENTS

Speaking at industry-focused events is a great way to increase your exposure and your authority.

Find out what events your ideal customers attend and offer to present at them.

If your specialty is some new, hot, technology it can be of real interest to people and you could find yourself in demand.

You will usually get much better engagement if you can address some industry pain points and/or be a bit controversial or contrary. Don't be afraid to make some bold statements. That's how people will remember you.

SPEAKING ENGAGEMENT TIPS

There are lots of good books about speaking in public so invest in learning more about what makes a good speech.

Assuming you're permitted to do it, hold a Q&A session at the end of your talk. This is a great way to engage with your audience and demonstrate your expertise.

You *must* have a Call to Action (CTA) at the end of your talk.

When you're invited to speak at somebody else's event you will not be in control of capturing the attendee's contact details. Some event organizers will share these details with you and others won't.

> *Never speak at an event without having some mechanism*
> *to capture attendee details.*

Regardless, you want to make sure that you capture details of as many of these people yourself so that you can build up your mailing list.

So, offer to give away a white paper or another lead magnet in return for them giving you their email address. You could also ask them to leave their business card in return for receiving the white paper, etc.

Make yourself available for follow-up questions and discussions outside the room or over lunch after your talk. If you've delivered a great talk, you could find yourself sitting down with some great prospects who want to hear more from you. One outcome could be that you get a chance to present your full core story to their organization.

TESTIMONIALS AND CASE STUDIES

BUILDING TRUST

The most important goal in marketing a professional services business is to build trust. if your marketing doesn't generate trust, it won't generate customers.

Two of the most persuasive ways of building trust and converting prospects into customers are testimonials and case studies.

TESTIMONIALS

> *A written declaration certifying to a person's character,
> conduct, or qualifications, or the value, excellence, etc., of
> a thing; a letter or written statement of recommendation.*

www.dictionary.com

In other words, testimonials are short pieces of feedback from customers or other parties describing their thoughts and experiences of a company, a person, a product, or a service.

Testimonials are a very powerful marketing tool because:

- They build trust. When your customers rave about what your product has done for them or about the great service you gave, they tell the story of a positive experience with your products/services and business.

- They aren't "salesy." Testimonials aren't written in your "voice"; they are written in the "voice" of the testimonial giver. They stand out as truthful and impartial accounts of how well your product works or how great your service is.

- They overcome skepticism. A good testimonial has the power to convince even the most skeptical prospect that your product or service really made a difference in your customer's life—and you can help them, too.

TESTIMONIAL TIPS

Once you know a customer is satisfied always ask for a testimonial. If you don't ask, you're less likely to get one. Ask if they would be prepared to give a video testimonial. If a written testimonial is powerful, then a video testimonial is many times as powerful.

Ask the customer if they will be prepared to take a call from a prospect when appropriate. I regularly had customers take calls from interested prospects. In nearly all cases we ended up working with the prospect.

Be careful not to abuse the customer's willingness to take calls. Use it sparingly and for really important deals. Most customers won't mind taking a couple of calls each year, but they will start to back off if you do it every week or every month.

The more that you can get quantifiable stats into the testimonial the stronger it will be. So, for example, if you can get the customer to say that they saved $xxx or that they increased revenue by x%, then it makes it a more powerful testimonial.

Along with the testimonial, make sure to add the person's name, job title, and company. If they'll permit it, include a photo of the person. All of this helps establish the authenticity of the person giving the testimonial.

Make sure to post the testimonial on your website and push it out through your social media channels. Publicize your testimonials to prospects in your sales pipeline. It adds more credibility to your sales efforts.

In the startup phase of your business, before you have any customers, you can use testimonials that you've personally received in previous positions/roles.

If you don't have any, then go ask some people you've worked for previously if they could give you a testimonial.

Be careful not to say anything that might cause an issue with a previous employer. The best way to do this is to have the testimonial focus on your capabilities, your integrity, your skills, etc.

CASE STUDIES

Case studies are a great way to demonstrate to prospects how valuable your products or services are.

They go beyond simple testimonials by showing real-life examples of how you were able to satisfy your customers' needs and help them accomplish their goals.

With great case studies, you will be able to highlight your successes in a way that will help convert prospects into customers.

Case studies appeal to people because they tell a story that the reader can relate to. And when the reader relates to a case study it increases your credibility as an organization that can help solve their problems.

Case studies are also great for SEO. You can pepper them with relevant keywords and phrases so that they appear high up in searches by your ideal customers.

Case studies are a fundamental part of a content marketing strategy and they make great collateral for your sales and marketing campaigns. Potential customers get an in-depth look at what it's like working with your product or service, thus reducing uncertainty.

CASE STUDY TIPS

A case study is all about the customer's experience of working with you. It is focused on the customer, not on you. Tell a story as a journey from a problem situation to a better situation.

When writing a case study, make the customer the hero of the story.

Make sure you have a strong, attention-grabbing headline. A great headline will massively increase the chances that people will read your copy so spend time crafting it. Make the story compelling to your target audience. Include numbers and metrics that demonstrate how your product or service helped the customer.

Supplement the study with quotes, photos, charts, etc., to increase readability and interest. Make sure that the copy leaves the reader with a clear understanding of the outcomes they can expect if they work with you.

If the customer will agree to a video interview, then that would maximize the effectiveness of the case study. It would be worth spending some bucks on getting a video testimonial.

Get the case study designed and branded to make it look professional. If the study looks professional, it will create a professional look to your company. Use a site like www.fiverr.com to source a person to format it.

Make sure the case study is easily readable. If people find it difficult to read then they are more likely to bin it. As a general rule short paragraphs, bullets and lists, quote blocks, charts and graphs, etc., help improve readability. Check the readability against the Coleman-Liau index or Flesch Kincaid Grade Level.

PERSONAL GROWTH

TO GROW THE COMPANY YOU MUST GROW

A key part of the strategy of growing your company is for you to personally grow your skills.

Nobody will expect you to know everything about business when you start, but you must be open to learning new skills. You should aim to become a lifelong learner in all the skills of a business owner.

You should view the start of your business as the beginning of a journey that will transform you into an even better version of yourself. Set yourself a goal to learn more about key functions such as entrepreneurship, leadership and management, sales, marketing, negotiation, customer service, etc.

Be prepared to invest some of your profits in learning more about running a business.

"An investment in knowledge always pays the best interest."

Benjamin Franklin

There are many ways you can learn new skills. Sources of new skills include:

- Books and Audiobooks
- Videos/TED Talks/YouTube
- Podcasts
- Blogs & Newletters
- Technical and Industry events
- Online courses

I invested heavily in books and audiobooks all through my career as a CEO. My phone was always loaded with business podcasts that I listened to while traveling.

I made a point of going to at least one major event each year. These were invaluable for keeping me in touch with our market and for spotting upcoming trends.

We also brought in consultants and advisors when we felt we needed additional skills or knowledge.

The bottom line is this: Investing in yourself is a big investment in your business. The better the leader you become the more successful your business will be.

SUMMARY

IT'S TIME TO DECIDE

In this book, I've covered the most important aspects of launching and running a profitable software development business. I hope that I have inspired you to start your own software business and build a new future for yourself, a future where there are no upper limits on your earnings and where you can create real wealth and financial freedom for you and your loved ones.

I started my business without having much of this knowledge. I had to learn it as I went along. I ran the business as CEO for more than 20 years and I was still learning new things every week.

After reading this book you will have an advantage I never had. You will be armed with a level of knowledge that few startup business owners will have.

You will know how to launch your business without taking on any debt and you will know the strategies and tactics that will help you grow to seven figures and more.

You will know how to operate the business profitably and how to scale your business and build a valuable company that can provide a wonderful future for you and your family.

Now it's time to make a decision.

Are you happy to continue following somebody else's dream and keep making them wealthy? Or is it time to design your new life plan and take control of your future by working for the best boss ever? *You!*

"If you don't design your own life plan, chances are you'll fall into someone else's plan. And guess what they have planned for you? Not much."

Jim Rohn

www.ingramcontent.com/pod-product-compliance
Lightning Source LLC
Chambersburg PA
CBHW051047050326
40690CB00006B/628